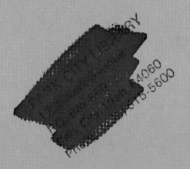

INVENT RADIUM
OR I'LL PULL YOUR HAIR

Invent Radium

OR I'LL PULL YOUR HAIR

DORIS DRUCKER

THE UNIVERSITY OF CHICAGO PRESS

CHICAGO AND LONDON

Doris Drucker was born in Cologne, Germany, and studied law and economics at the London School of Economics, Kiel University, and Frankfurt University. After her arrival in the United States, she received an M.S. in physics from Farleigh Dickinson University and conducted scientific market research as an independent contractor for several decades. In 1996, she founded RSQ, a company to manufacture and market a voice volume monitor invented by herself and a partner. A board member of several nonprofit organizations, she now lives in California.

The stanza from the "Lorelei" song is reproduced from *Poems of Heinrich Heine,* trans. Louis Untermeyer (New York: Heritage Press, 1957), p. 85.

The University of Chicago Press, Chicago 60637 ¶ The University of Chicago Press, Ltd., London ¶ © 2004 by The University of Chicago ¶ All rights reserved. Published 2004 ¶ Printed in the United States of America
13 12 11 10 09 08 07 06 05 04   1 2 3 4 5
ISBN: 0-226-16503-5 (cloth)

Drucker, Doris.
   Invent radium or I'll pull your hair / Doris Drucker.
       p.   cm.
   ISBN 0-226-16503-5 (hardcover : alk. paper)
   1. Drucker, Doris.   2. Drucker, Peter Ferdinand, 1909–.   3. Women—United States—Biography.   4. German Americans—Biography.   5. Germany—Biography.   I. Title.
CT275.D8754 A3 2004
300'.92—dc22

                                                                                        2003017880

⊗ The paper used in this publication meets the minimum requirements of the American National Standard for Information Sciences—Permanence of Paper for Printed Library Materials, ANSI Z39.48-1992.

To the memory of my mother,
CLARA SCHMITZ

Contents

THE BLACK HAT 1

WORLD WAR I 5

THE SERVANTS 13

THE ORIGINAL INFORMATION TECHNOLOGY 18

THE ANCESTORS 21

THE CHILDREN 28

MY MOTHER'S MARRIAGE 31

THE GERMAN DEFEAT 41

THE FRENCH ARRIVE 44

KOENIGSTEIN 47

THE SOCIAL ORDER 51

A WIDER HORIZON 57

THE INFLATION YEARS 63

BACK TO SCHOOL   69

MY FATHER   77

BOOKS   81

BACK TO ST. MORITZ   83

THE SISTERS   86

THE FLOBERTS   92

THE SCHILLER SCHOOL   95

TRAVEL   100

SKI TRIPS   106

MY INTELLECTUAL JOURNEY   110

THE FACTS OF LIFE   114

FRANKFURT   121

TUNBRIDGE WELLS   131

THE SETTLEMENT HOUSE   139

A FORMER THIEF   144

CLIMBING THE SOCIAL LADDER   147

A MARRIAGE PROPOSAL   151

THE WARBURG INSTITUTE   156

IN FRANCE   162

LA BOHÊME   167

BACK TO THE LAW   173

MEETING PETER AGAIN   180

A DINNER PARTY   182

POSTSCRIPT   185

THE BLACK HAT

$\mathcal{M}$y great-uncle Albert's funeral in the summer of 1932 got me out of Germany for good. He had been dying for several months. During the long ordeal, his wife, my great-aunt Flora, had plenty of time to think about his funeral. On the morning her husband breathed his last she summoned my mother, her niece, and gave out orders: "Everybody to be in black—dress, shoes, stockings, gloves, and hat—not the younger children of course, but definitely Doris—she is old enough." "But she does not have a black hat," objected my mother, "she has a blue hat to go with her winter coat, and a yellow straw hat for the summer." "Then buy her one," demanded Aunt Flora. "What?" cried my mother, "Just for one funeral?" "She can save it for yours," said Aunt Flora acidly. She was furious that her dear departed was not deemed worthy of a new black hat.

The women kept on arguing; my mother was adamant. At last, Aunt Flora proposed a solution: "Doris can wear my maidservant's black hat." "Over my dead body!" said my mother—perhaps not the most tactful words considering that poor Uncle Albert's dead body was lying in the bedroom a few yards away. "Gretchen has lice." "She has no lice," said Aunt Flora categorically, "I would have seen them." "She has too," persisted my mother. "She does not," said Aunt Flora. "Come with me, I will show you." The two women went out into the kitchen for proof. A slatternly maid was washing dishes by the sink. "Please stop what you are doing, Gretchen," commanded Aunt Flora, "and bring that footstool from the corner over here." Gretchen withdrew her red arms from the soapy water and dried them on her apron. She picked up the footstool and held it in front of her. "Over here," said Aunt Flora. "Put it down and sit down." Gretchen complied, waiting for further instructions. Aunt Flora and my mother moved closer and peered down on the girl's skull, which was overlaid by thin strands of dirty-blond hair. "No lice," said Aunt Flora triumphantly. "Not so fast," objected my mother, "I want to make sure. They could be hiding." The women kept on scrutinizing Gretchen's head. Finally, my mother conceded: "No lice." "I told you so," said Aunt Flora. "You can get up, Gretchen." The servant girl wiped her nose on the end of her sleeve and wordlessly went back to the sink. The two women returned to the living room. I wore Gretchen's shapeless black hat to the funeral; afterwards I washed my hair with strong soap.

Poor dead Great-Uncle Albert! For my mother, her siblings, and their many cousins, he had been a formative influence: he dissuaded them from making undesirable marriages and found them what he considered suitable spouses. If a young man got into trouble by gambling or by impregnating a young servant girl, it was Uncle Albert who arranged for the boy to be shipped off to America "to further his education"—an indefinite and, it was to be hoped, drawn-out process which circumvented scandal. But by the time we, the next generation, came along, Uncle Albert was too old and worn out to brood over, let alone solve, our problems. During his lifetime I regarded him as just one of a great many elderly strolling players on the stage on which my childhood played itself out. He was a benevolent spectator, as so many old men are, who was beyond worrying how we youngsters would turn out. Yet the accident of his death had a decisive influence on my future. Quite possibly, I might not have had a future at all had he not died that very day.

Returning from the cemetery, we were overtaken by a band of brownshirted, jackbooted Nazis marching down the street to the Horst Wessel Lied, their venomous hate song. The Nazis started to show off the superiority of the master race by hurtling bricks and stones in all directions. The onlookers responded with enthusiastic Heil Hitlers, Germany Awake, and Death to the Jews. Broken glass from street lamps and store windows crashed onto the pavement, people screamed, and we ducked into a doorway to wait until the commotion was over. We were not particularly alarmed: in the summer of 1932, riots occurred almost every day. If it was not the Nazis going on a rampage, it was the Communists. Nonetheless, a Dutch relative who had come to Frankfurt for the funeral was appalled by the pandemonium. "How can you be so sanguine?" he chided us. "This is not going to end well. If the Nazis come to power there will be war. Leave while you can." "Leave Frankfurt? How can we? Our homes, our families, our business, our jobs—everything we have is tied up here," objected the mourners. "But what about you, Doris?" said the Dutchman. "Nothing holds you here. Come to Holland. I'll get you a job in my company so that you can support yourself. Didn't you say that your J.D. thesis was on a subject in international law? Well, you can work on that in Holland just as well. Or even better because you can make use of the resources at the library of the World Court of Justice at The Hague. I am sure your job will allow you plenty of spare time. And if the situation in Germany should improve, you can always go back and finish your studies in Frankfurt." My thesis adviser, who happened to be one of the judges at The Hague Court, thought it was an excellent idea. Three weeks later I went to Holland. Politics had little to do with my decision. I did not share the Dutchman's dire prognosis for the future of Germany, but his suggestion was a welcome opportunity to get out from under my mother's thumb. Having lived abroad during the first two years of my university studies, I had tasted freedom. At home in Frankfurt, my mother, who held the purse strings, controlled every aspect of my life, from the clothes I was to wear to the husband she was going to choose for me—or was she tracking an ideal son-in-law for herself? The opportunity to flee that depressing domestic atmosphere was too good to pass up, and the educational aspect was a perfect justification for getting away.

Little did I know that my departure was not a temporary escape; it became a permanent severance from Germany. I have been back several times, but I never lived there again. The atrocious Nazi time all but severed any emotional attachments to my homeland; however, the memories of my childhood and youth stayed on. They were not always happy in the sense of being idyllic or harmonious. But they are uniquely my very own, and nothing that happened ever after can replace or obscure them.

$\mathcal{L}$ ike every young child, I spent the first two or three years of my life outside Time. There was no Present, because every Present is defined by a Past and a Future. Life was a number of still photographs, of events that are not subject to the dimensions of Time. Space was real; you touch the door, the boundaries of a room, and the things that are in it, things that are standing still, and things that move.

"Quick," my mother called, "the Zeppelin." A large silvery object floated through the air, way up, higher than all the houses. The people in the street cried: "Look at the people in the sky waving to us from the Zeppelin!" "I saw the Zeppelin," I told Old Anna, who was my nursemaid. "So you did," she said. "What did it look like to you?" "It was a big bird," I said, "bigger than the swans in the fairy tale that flew away with the little girl."

I also saw an automobile. Automobiles had been invented years before, but they rarely came to the small village where we spent the summer. "Look at the automobile," exclaimed my mother, "it moves by itself." Actually, it did not move at all. It sat in the middle of the village. Two men in strange clothes ran around what looked like a cart and tried to take it apart, or anyway, they tore off a lot of pieces and then put them back on. We watched them run around for a while. I wondered why it took so long for the horses to be fed and watered; eventually a man came with horses and they pulled the cart away. I knew it all along—you needed horses to get any cart to move.

The Zeppelin and the automobile appeared and disappeared in my hazy world.

Once I was in a large building with an immensely high ceiling. There was a peculiar musty smell. Old Anna knelt down next to me. Then she got up and went away. When she returned she had her hands folded across her stomach. Years later I was told that Anna, who was supposed to take me for my daily "airing," always stopped for Mass in the Cologne Cathedral. What I remember as a singular event is probably a composite of many such visits.

Another time I was in a narrow room that kept shaking, but the houses and the trees outside were making even more of a commotion; they were whizzing by the windows. My mother and Old Anna sat on benches across from each other. Old Anna had a large basket next to her. I climbed up on the bench to look what was inside. My mother and Old Anna cried as one: "No, no, you are hurting your sister!" What was a sister, and what was it doing in a basket? Then the haze enveloped me again, and I knew no more who or where I was.

The clouds opened again when I saw my mother and many other people run up and down a short steep hill which led from our house into the woods. While they were running they shouted "Mobilization!" and many more people came out of their houses and joined them, and they all kept running up and down that hill. I was bewildered; I had never seen grown-up people run. They always walked quite sedately because they had to carry things: baskets, sacks, pails or bundles of firewood, scythes or rakes, and, of course, babies. I did not know what "mobilization" meant. Did it have anything to do with an automobile? There was none in sight. We all kept running until the town crier came along and rang his big bell to make the people stop and listen to a long letter that he read to them.

Then we were in a large room with a table set for a meal. Many people were bustling around, pushing chairs and creating a lot of unrest. An old man with a beard came in and sat down, and then everybody else sat down too. My mother and the other people ate in silence. I kept looking at all the strangers around the table. My baby sister in a highchair was banging a spoon against a plate. Suddenly the old man, my grandfather, fixed his gaze on me and addressed me in a threatening voice: "Why are you staring at me like that with your big saucer eyes?" I didn't know what I had done to make him so angry, and I began to cry loudly. My grandfather threw his napkin down and jumped out of his seat. "I can't stand that noise—are we going to have that every day while they are here?" My mother and her sisters whisked us children away, and until we were ten years old or so we no longer ate with the family, except three or four times a year at festive occasions.

My grandfather's outburst happened on the day of our arrival at his home in Mainz, "for the duration," after my father had been called up for the army. Before that, my parents and my baby sister and I lived in Cologne, which was my father's hometown and where he was in business. After her arranged marriage at age twenty to a man for whom she did not care in the least, my mother was determined to dislike everything about Cologne. And when my father—and his income—disappeared at the outbreak of the War, she closed up the household and moved with us children back to her parents' home. This was supposed to last only for a few months—until "our heroic boys" had beaten the French and the British and the Belgians and the Russians and everybody in between. Nobody could have foreseen that our visit would stretch out into a four-year stay, until the First World War ended with the decisive defeat of Germany.

Worse for me than banishment to the *Katzentisch* (literally, "cats' table," meaning a low table in a corner where little children ate by themselves) was this traumatic ejection out of my shell, where things happened in no particular sequence. Suddenly there was time, cause, and consequence. In self-defense, I constructed a timeless world inside me that I did not have to share with anybody. My family, the servants, and the few other people I knew all fitted in, and so did the streetcars, the Rhine River, and the flocks of birds that flew around the church steeples. All that had a real and figurative existence inside me. What or whom I did not like was left standing outside and disconnected. The only problem was how to get the War into my inner space—the soldiers and the horses and, above all, the huge cannons. They did belong, of course; the War was our natural environment in which everything took place. Beyond it there was nothing. At night I fell asleep trying to solve this problem. The War within me and around me was everywhere, all over the world. War was part of the universe, a permanent configuration that sometimes moved from one country to another. We did not know that when the War settled anywhere it devastated the country and smashed everything to pieces, trees and houses, people and animals—everything. How could we have known? Mainz, so close to the French border, had been invaded many times by the French during the past centuries. But the shot-up buildings had been repaired, and the only remnants of the Napoleonic wars were the many French words sprinkled throughout the local language. Germany, the aggressor, had carried the First World War into France and Belgium, ravaging these countries and ferociously tearing up the landscape at an unspeakable cost of lives. But for now our houses were kept standing, the trains were running, and children played in the streets. We sang patriotic songs, assuring the fatherland and ourselves that the "Watch on the Rhine" would stand fast and hold the enemy at bay.

Sometimes the sounds and sights of war came closer; for us children they were interesting, non-threatening diversions. Outside town we lay on the ground and listened to the booming cannons shooting off round after round on the Western Front some sixty or seventy miles away. We stood by the window and watched a small plane circling lazily over the rooftops. Suddenly it dropped a small dark object and there was a loud bang. My mother came into the room and said we should get away from the window.

Night air raids were more interesting; from the beginning of the War on we had blackouts to shield us from air attacks. However, the attempts to leave the enemy literally in the dark were quite ineffectual. A city like Mainz, at the confluence of the Rhine and

Main rivers, could easily be seen from the air when the waters reflected the moonlight. So whenever a French plane approached at night and dropped a bomb or two, the sirens began to blare and we were bundled up in blankets and carried down to the cellar, where all the tenants were assembled. We were fascinated to see the tasseled nightcaps on the men's heads and the ladies' hairpieces in unfamiliar disarray. What was even more astonishing was the temporary suspension of rules of behavior. The tenants from the first floor, a retired major and his wife, actually deigned to talk to us civilians. Under normal circumstances such familiarity would have been most unusual; in the pecking order of Germany before the War, a member of the Officer Corps was a near-deity, living according to a code of behavior that excluded communication with ordinary people.

Of course, the cellar shelter was only for the gentry; the servants were considered dispensable in their attic chambers. Nevertheless, the gentry would have been quite dismayed if the maids had been bombed out and unable to serve breakfast as usual the next morning.

I do not remember that the planes did any damage—certainly not in comparison with the inhuman onslaught of the Second World War. At least, the adults thought that the invasion of our airspace was just an annoyance, and quite insignificant considering our army's alleged gains on all fronts. Swept off their feet by waves of patriotism, everybody believed that victory was all but assured, and the pins on the war map in the hall were triumphantly moved outward, toward France and Belgium in the West and toward Poland and Russia in the East, wishfully marking our forward positions in enemy country. When people met in the street they called out the names of cities or of battles: Verdun, Lille, Rheims, and the Marne. We did not understand what it was all about, but like all children we were happy when our families were happy.

One summer day we were in a small park where women met for a cup of substitute coffee while their children played in a sandbox. In a gazebo a small orchestra of weary old men played war tunes. Suddenly my mother, waving a newspaper, summoned my sister and myself to her table. "Quick," she said excitedly, "both of you run and tell everybody that Warschau has fallen." Even if I had known that Warschau (Warsaw) was a city in Poland, her command would have made no sense. Things fall down or people fall down: perhaps I misunderstood; "Warschau" sounded similar to "Waschfrau"—washerwoman—ah, that's what probably happened. "Was she hurt?" I asked. "Don't ask stupid questions," said my mother, "run and do as you are told." We dashed off to the next table singing out loud: "The Waschfrau has fallen." The ladies looked uncomprehending: "Who?" "The Waschfrau," we repeated, "you know, Frau Haashohl!" The ladies still could not understand. "What's this about, and who is Frau Haashohl?" I knew I had to follow my mother's orders, but how could I convey her message? "Frau Haashohl," I said once again, "the asshole—that's what Uncle Carl called her." The ladies gasped—but at last I had been able to communicate. So we continued skipping the preliminaries and just told one and all that the asshole had fallen.

One day we came home from a walk and found a soldier in the living room. "Come in!" he cried. "Remember me? I'm your dad." We stood by the door and looked at our mother. "Come, sit on my lap," said the soldier. "No, no!" cried my mother. "It's all right," said the soldier, "I have been through delousing." Dutifully we moved toward him; he showed us a photo of himself on a horse by way of an explanation of what he did in the War. In fact, he was a paramedic who had to pick the horribly mutilated dead and half-dead off the barbed wire strung between the opposing trenches. Like all soldiers on the Western Front, he lived for years like a rat, and with rats as steady companions, in the muddy trenches that ran for miles through Belgium and northern France. It rains a lot in that part of the world; for weeks on end the soldiers lived in dampness, unable even to change into dry socks, having nothing to eat except mildewy rations. Day and night they were exposed to the unceasing noise of gunfire and artillery shells close by: hell on earth. But my father never talked of what he had seen, then or later on. And when his furlough was over, his disappearance was as inexplicable as his arrival had been.

My Uncle Carl's furlough was far more colorful. One fine day he appeared out of the blue at the head of a train of hand-pulled carts, each of which was loaded with cages of chicken and geese, sheep and goats. "Carl," cried my grandmother, "what is all this?" "Liberated from the Balkans," said Carl cheerfully. He told us that he had traveled for five days in a cattle car with the entire menagerie, feeding and watering "his" animals and protecting them from other "liberators." On his arrival in Mainz he had hired the carts at the railroad station. "You walked through the whole town with that zoo?" asked my grandmother incredulously. "Sure did," said Carl. My grandmother was appalled; people would talk. "Let them," said Carl, "but at least you'll have some meat to eat."

We were thrilled with the small zoo, which was kept for the time being in the cobblestone yard. We rode around on the sheep and fed the chickens and watched the animals disappear one by one. We overheard the adults saying, "Don't tell the children," but we were so delighted with the meat on our plates that we refrained from asking where it came from.

The Allies' blockade of Germany cut off all food imports; rice, grains, meat, tea, coffee, oranges, and everything that was not grown at home disappeared. And when the German peasants were put into uniform, domestic food production fell off sharply. Without tractors or other farm machinery, women and children could not manage the backbreaking work: ploughing was still done with oxen, grains were cut with scythes, and hay bales were lifted by hand into the barn lofts. We ate potatoes and turnips and bread that was half sawdust. Our milk was almost transparent because it was diluted with so much water. Though I did not mind the quality, I did mind that there was so little of everything. We were not starving, but we were always hungry.

To supplement the meager rations we went foraging in the summer and fall. In vacant lots and on the side of the roads out of town we picked stinging nettles and thistles which were cooked as vegetables; rose hips that were seeded and made into jam; bramble leaves that were dried and used for tea; and chicory for coffee. Unfortunately, most of these weeds were—and undoubtedly still are—richly endowed with thorns and spines which went right through our thin gloves. "You poor children," said the aunts, "you have never eaten a banana or an orange. Before the War . . ."

Before the War meant for us an unfathomable past. Was it then that giants lurked in the hills, Red Riding Hood went to visit her grandmother, and the animals in Aesop's fables talked to one another? How could we ever understand that "before the War" meant a time that came later, much later, than the prehistoric fairy tales? For all we knew, the War had imperceptibly evolved from time immemorial and would now stay with us forever. One day my mother went around with a grim face muttering to herself, "America has come in—that's the end for us." We children did not believe it, of course; reality and Grimm's fairy tales shared the same tense, and "the end" meant that "they lived happily ever after."

$\mathcal{T}$he outbreak of the War had overwhelmed my grandparents. They were not really old people—both were in their late fifties, but in those days people of that age were considered old, and they felt old and entitled to enjoy serene sunset years. Now they were faced with the departure of their only son (my uncle Carl) and of half a dozen close family members into the army, not to mention general disorder, food rationing, the restrictions imposed on everyday life, and the arrival of my mother with two little children, who had to be taken in. Moreover, two young daughters, Margret and Anne, were still living at home.

It cannot have been easy for my mother either to be a guest in her parents' home, although her relief at being away from Cologne and her husband probably more than compensated for the drawbacks of the situation. Besides, there was none of that "two women in one kitchen" syndrome. My grandmother was an excellent and well-organized hausfrau, whereas my mother loathed any domestic activity. It suited both of them that my mother would take care of us children and my grandmother would run the household, assisted by a full complement of servants: a cook, a parlor maid, at least two undermaids, a cleaning woman to "do the floors," and a laundress every other week. An ironing girl followed the laundress the next day, and a seamstress came for mending things. Every morning a barber appeared to shave my grandfather, and a hairdresser to arrange my grandmother's hair. When my grandmother went marketing, she was accompanied by one of the maids with a hamper to carry the food. When she traveled—as a matter of fact, when anybody in the family traveled—a porter and a cart were summoned to bring the luggage to the railway station. The travelers followed in a hired horse-drawn cab. A maid in charge of coats and other paraphernalia usually accompanied the travelers on the train.

By today's standards, it seems preposterous that a middle-class—or what the Germans called *gut buergerliche*—family would employ that many servants. However, compared to the twenty or more servants kept by aristocratic families—not counting coachmen, grooms, and stable boys—the total number of servants in my grandparents' household was not at all extravagant. One has to remember that all the chores we now do mechanically had to be done manually—by somebody. Hot water did not flow from any tap; water for washing clothes and dishes, not to mention personal hygiene, had to be heated on the wood-burning kitchen stove. Messages were not delivered over a telephone: they had to be hand-carried back and forth. Turning a switch did not produce light—the ceiling fixtures in the living room and dining room came on only after a maid had opened a valve and held a flame to the outflowing gas. Outside, a lamplighter made the rounds every evening and lit the streetlights one by one. In the morning he came back and extinguished them.

Although my grandparents' apartment was quite elegant by local standards, it had just one toilet and, separate from it, a bathroom with a bathtub and a sink. The bathroom was used only on Saturday nights, when a maid lit a fire under a water heater for the once-a-week ablutions. In between, everybody made do with a more or less perfunctory sponge bath. Every morning the maids carried hot water from the kitchen to the bedrooms to fill the water jugs and washbasins that stood on marble-topped chests of drawers. After the masters and mistresses had performed their superficial rubdowns, the maids carried the wash water away.

Laundering was by far the most exhausting chore. Even as a child I pitied the poor worn-out washerwoman. There were no washing machines. The laundress had to boil clothes in a huge cauldron, haul them out piece by piece with a long wooden stick, rinse them repeatedly in fresh water, and then carry them outside to "bleach in the sun." When my newly married grandmother arrived in Mainz in 1885, there was in the middle of town a grassy piece of land designated as a communal bleaching ground. (Today that piece of property is a heavily traveled street, still called "*Die Grosse Bleiche.*") Every other week my grandmother walked to that place with two of the maids, who carried hampers full of damp clothes. Having seen to it that the linens were properly spread out on the grass, my grandmother returned home with one maid. The other one was left behind to guard the clothes—not so much from thieves as from mischievous street urchins. At night the supposedly bleached clothes were brought home, rinsed, wrung out again, and carried—imagine those loads!—to a loft in the attic, where they were hung on lines to dry.

Ironing was hardly less strenuous. Fat iron wedges, heated until they were red-hot, were shoved into the hollow interior of heavy pressing irons. There were no temperature controls. The ironing girl touched a wetted finger against the sole of the iron. If it sizzled, the temperature was right. Often the girl's fingertips were so callused from all the testing that she could no longer judge heat gradations, with the result that she burned the clothes. Of course, there was no wash-and-wear. Everything was made from natural fibers—linen, wool, or cotton—and everything was pleated, embroidered, and beribboned and had to be pressed very carefully.

Because there was no refrigeration, perishables had to be shopped for every day—no small job for a family of seven plus five or so servants. In the summer, my grandmother would sometimes summon the iceman, who lugged a heavy ice block upstairs and slung it into a semi-insulated icebox. Food was piled on top and around the ice until it melted and drained into a bowl at the bottom.

In his recent book *From Dawn to Decadence,* the historian Jacques Barzun states that past achievements in the political, social, and artistic sphere were possible only because servants freed the leading spirits to do the work: writers such as Dickens or Balzac could not have produced their phenomenal literary output without servants at their beck and call.

In the middle-class society in which I grew up, it would have been unthinkable for anybody in the family to do "maids' work"; the only exception was an occasional cooking bout, which could be described as a hobby. Anything else would have been downright immoral. What would happen to the poor if somebody took over the servants' roles?

We never, ever, made our own beds, and until I was in high school, I did not know anybody among our acquaintances who did. A classmate, recounting some catastrophe in her family, mentioned that it had forced her mother to make the beds for a week. "Your mother made the beds?" we asked incredulously. It must have been a severe crisis.

For all their labors, the servants earned a pittance, but at least they were housed and fed; the alternative was to starve at home in a village. Under German law, the oldest son inherited the family farm when his father died. This was not discrimination against the younger children; the law was designed to prevent the division of a small holding into unsustainable small plots for each of the children. In theory, the heir was to pay off his siblings, but in practice there was no money. To survive at all, the uneducated young peasant boys and girls had to hire themselves out as servants. Girls who had gotten themselves "into trouble" in the village became surrogate breast-feeders for women who could not or did not want to breast-feed their own newborns. Shortly after the girl had given birth, either she or her family gave the new baby away to an "Angelmaker," a woman who starved the little children in her care to death, and the young mother was hired out as a wet nurse. Her employers plied her with beer and all the rich food you can think of, to make her milk and the baby fatter and fatter, which, in those days, was a sign of enviable health. Well-to-do mothers preferred to have their babies nourished by a wet nurse. It was much more convenient than to have to be on tap around the clock. Besides, breast-feeding was considered to be degrading: it made you into a sort of milch cow. And for birth mothers who could not nurse their babies, a substitute was almost a necessity because there was no such thing as a formula to feed newborns.

Many years later, when the name Freud had entered the vocabulary of the educated and especially the semi-educated, people traced all kinds of real or imaginary psychological and physiological afflictions back to their wet nurses. As an adult, did you suffer from rheumatism, drug addiction, hypochondria? Sure—it was all the wet nurse's fault: through her milk, you became predisposed to this disorder or that affliction, and so on, ad absurdum. By the time we were born, fashions had changed, and women were encouraged to breast-feed their babies. My mother went at it vigorously because, as she told me later, "I wanted to override the bad genes your father has contributed to your existence."

THE ORIGINAL INFORMATION TECHNOLOGY

*D*omestic servants worked hard. There were no eight-hour days and none of the fringe benefits we now take for granted. On the other hand, being "in service" had definite advantages. There were more marriageable young men in the city than in the village, and a benevolent mistress, like my grandmother, would help the young girls find suitable husbands. Moreover, instead of remaining isolated villagers, the peasant girls who went into domestic service became a part, albeit a minor one, of urban society. They were nodes in a far-flung information network through which news and gossip flowed. Servants knew everything about everybody, and especially all the secret skeletons in their employers' closets. It was impossible to hide anything from them. They did not have to listen or look through keyholes. They absorbed, almost by osmosis, everything that went on behind closed doors. My grandmother switched to French—"Tais-toi, les domestiques!"—when somebody inadvertently mentioned a subject which the family did not want to be spread around, and everybody shut up until the servant had left the room. It did not make the slightest difference. Within five minutes, the entire kitchen staff knew.

For servants, gossip was like money in the bank, a marketable commodity, which at the very least earned them the employers' goodwill. If a family was informed of an ongoing rumor or of the likely consequences of a family member's imprudence, it might be possible to contain the damage before the matter became a scandal. Servants had good reasons to protect "their" family; any threat to the family's well-being, reputation, or general stability was also a threat to their own future.

"If I were the *gnaedige Frau* (an appellation that is roughly comparable to the Spanish *señora*), I would not call in Dr. C.," said the parlor maid. "Why not? He has been our physician for years." "Yes, but lately his drug addiction has become so much worse that he is sometimes half asleep and doesn't know what he is doing." "How do you know?" asked the mistress. "Well, the C.'s' cook's niece, who is in service at the D.'s, told our Hedwig that Dr. C.'s arm is full of needle marks where he shoots himself with morphine. And then he passes out a lot." "Thank you, Louise," said the mistress, "I am glad you told me." But for Louise's timely information, the mistress would never have known.

Many years later, when I was at the university but still living at home, the parlor maid became keenly interested in the company I kept. She assumed that in all likelihood my future husband would come from that group. Whenever fellow students, girls or boys, came to our house, she inspected the labels inside the coats they had hung on a rack in the hall. Then she reported to my mother, who relayed Johanna's reasoned opinion that "Miss Doris ought not to associate with those *Herrn und Fraeulein Studenten.* They are a grubby lot. Their clothes come from really cheap stores—no good." "Johanna is absolutely right," said my mother. "You will ruin all prospects for a proper marriage if you run around with those dowdy people."

I took it for granted that the world revolved around me, and that the servants were there to keep the carousel from stopping. Not only children, but adults as well, considered it akin to a law of nature that servants were here to serve their masters. Life without servants was unimaginable. I know of one extreme case where that point of view became a death sentence. In 1939, when the Nazi persecution of the Jews was in full swing, a German Jewish woman received a much-coveted visa to go to England. A British couple, her sponsors, wanted to hire her as a housemaid. The woman refused to accept the job. "What if somebody who knew me saw me mop the kitchen floor?" she protested. I heard later that she perished in Auschwitz. When Lenin was exiled to Siberia in the 1890s, he took, of course, servants with him. Even after World War II it was not unusual for a servant to accompany refugees: my cousin Mariana's family, fleeing from advancing Russians in East Germany, crisscrossed the countryside accompanied, of course, by their cook.

I remember a retired senior government official and his wife who lost all their pension income during the Great Inflation. They had become as poor as the proverbial church mice. Finally, they had to choose between buying fuel for cooking or paying for a daily hairdresser for Mrs. X. They opted for the hairdresser, although it meant that the pitiful old couple had to go every day into the woods to carry home a few sticks of firewood.

𝕸y grandfather once told me that he had traced the family lineage back to Emperor Frederick the Great's reign around 1780, but I never saw documents to prove it. His ancestors came from Lahnstein, a lovely little town in the Rhine valley. Sometime in the early nineteenth century the family moved to Idstein, a small village in the Taunus woods and some twenty or thirty miles distant from Mainz. The Lahnsteins were farmers, although peasants would be a better description. It was a hard life; up at dawn and out to work in the fields. My great-grandmother bore fifteen or sixteen children, of whom my grandfather, I believe, was number twelve. At the age of forty-five or fifty both the great-grandfather and the great-grandmother were worn out and died.

Unlike their counterparts in the United States, European farmers lived not on their land but in a village, which offered some protection against the bandits and marauders who used to roam and plunder all over Europe. The Lahnsteins' house in Idstein was a typical peasant's homestead, with a barn adjoining the living quarters. We loved visiting there and living for a few days in an enchanting rural environment. We woke up to the sounds of the roosters, the stirring of the horses and cattle in the barn, and the creaking of the cartwheels, as people got ready to hitch up and drive out to the fields. A little later the shepherd walked by, blowing his flute and collecting all the sheep, which he and his dog were to take to pasture outside the village. The bleating of the noisy sheep had barely receded when the goose girl arrived to lead squawking geese to the village pond, where they were to waddle around all day. How my sister and I wished to be a goose girl and spend all our days in such an idyllic setting! Little did we know that the shepherd and the goose girl and their counterparts were usually orphans or retarded children whom the community maltreated and fed poorly in return for their labors.

We asked the aunts and uncles who still lived in the ancestral home how the large Lahnstein family could ever have fitted into the tiny house. They didn't—there were never more than eight or ten of them together at the same time. When a child reached the age of fourteen or fifteen, he or she was pushed out of the nest and sent away to America to earn a living and to make room for the next baby. I sometimes wonder what was more wrenching, the parents' sorrow at a parting forever, or the youngster's terror anticipating an unknowable future. There was no alternative except to starve on the small farm, where there never were enough crops to feed all those mouths. The youngsters were handed over to an agent who shepherded bands of emigrants to the ports of Hamburg or Bremen, where he stacked them, like so many pieces of cargo, in the steerage compartment of an America-bound ship. The passengers, mostly from landlocked Germany, had never seen the ocean; they were scared to death when the ship cast off. It was a miserable voyage; steerage was a large compartment without ventilation or any but the most primitive sanitary facilities. There was no privacy at all: the sick and the well, the crying children and the moaning adults huddled together in their common misery in that stinking space. At last, having landed and passed through the Immigration Station at Ellis Island, the youngsters were met by a stranger who claimed to be a relative—perhaps he really was— and delivered to an employer. The girls were sent into domestic service as scullery maids who lived in—"in" was usually a hole under the stairs or next to the coal cellar in the basement; the boys were hired out to a tradesman or a factory owner. Conscientious youngsters saved money to pay for the passage of the next-in-line sibling. By the time my grandfather's turn came, his older sisters had been married to well-off men, so that they were able to take their young brother on a trip to Niagara Falls before he had to start working. They wanted to show him the grandeur of the New World; unfortunately, their good intentions produced a totally unexpected reaction: instead of being awestruck, my grandfather was so scared of the torrents of water that he begged his sisters to let him go back to the gentle rivulets of Idstein.

Sometimes I have regretted his decision to return to Germany. If he had stayed in the United States, I thought, I would have been born an American citizen. I would have escaped the war and all the troubled times in Europe—a train of thought which overlooks the fact that my American grandfather would not have married my German grandmother, so that I, his descendant, would have turned out to be quite different from the individual that I am now.

I do not know whether my grandfather's experience dissuaded his younger siblings from emigrating to America. At any rate, when the baby of the family graduated from elementary school, his older brothers and sisters all chipped in to send him to high school and later to college to study medicine. Family gossip had it that he was a rather poor student, and that his professors were reluctant to give him the M.D. degree. Finally they let him graduate on condition that he practiced medicine only at a spa, where he could not do much damage. I do not know whether the story was true, but my great-uncle Ferdinand did settle in Wiesbaden, one of the many hot springs resorts which were extremely popular in eighteenth- and nineteenth-century Europe. There was Bath in England, Aix-les-Bains in France, Marienbad in Bohemia, Montecatini Terme in Italy, and a whole slew along the Rhine valley, from Baden-Baden to Homburg. Allegedly, each spa was beneficial for a specific malady. The waters in Bad Soden, a preferred gathering place of Russian grand dukes, were said to cure ear, nose, and throat diseases. Those in Bad Langenschwalbach—and an energetic, good-looking gynecologist—were known to cure infertility among young women. Bad Homburg was the domain of post-menopausal women who "took the cure," usually in the company of a nubile daughter or two. Karlsbad was famous for promoting intestinal "regularity."

There is a story, probably apocryphal, of a performance of Haydn's Symphony no. 25, the *Farewell* Symphony, in the Karlsbad Concert Hall. In the final Adagio, the score calls for the various instruments to disappear one by one. The wind players fold up their music stands and leave first; they are followed by the strings, and so on, until only two violins are left to play the last notes. Said one local concertgoer to his neighbor: "See, our good Karlsbad water."

Wiesbaden, which, unlike the other small-town spas, was a fair-sized city with plenty of diversions, attracted wealthy cure-seekers from America. Uncle Ferdinand not only looked after his patients' health but, jointly with Aunt Else, his sociable young wife, after their entertainment as well. The Mainz family was shocked by Else's bridge and tea parties—such extravagance! We liked her; in her coquettish silver mesh purse she always carried a small case full of candy which she doled out to us. And she always smelled so nice.

On his return from America, my grandfather and one of his cousins started a general store in Mainz which grew into a fair-sized business. Along the way, he married my grandmother, who was also a country girl. Her people were vintners in Ingelheim, which was a famous site for producing fine wines.

Although not as poor as the hardscrabble Lahnsteins in Idstein, my grandmother's family also lived a hand-to-mouth existence, depending on the right amount of sunshine and rain at the right time for a grape harvest that would make a great wine.

Along the German rivers, the Rhine, the Main and the Mosel, grapes were grown on steep terraced hills. Everything necessary to cultivate the plants had to be carried uphill; it was truly backbreaking work which culminated in the grape harvest in the fall. For weeks before, young boys armed with popguns sat all day in the vineyards to scare off any grape-stealing birds. At last, when the grapes were judged to be at their peak, all hands were summoned to pick. Men and women, young and old, climbed up and down those steep hills, with baskets on their backs and scissors in their hands. They moved through the rows and cut grape clusters as they went along. When their baskets were full they carried them downhill to unload and immediately climbed uphill again. Up and down, all day long, from dawn to dusk. I do not know how people got the idea that the grape harvest was a time for merrymaking, with pretty girls and their beaux dancing and stomping on the grapes in their bare feet. Everybody was exhausted at the end of the day.

When we visited we were not even allowed to go up into the vineyards, where we would have been in the way of the harvesters. Instead, we stood around in the farmyard where a blind donkey went round and round a huge stone basin full of cut grapes. The donkey was tied to an arm which operated a grape crusher in the basin. From time to time the juice was drawn off through a spigot and poured into oaken barrels. It was really quite boring. The adults were tense and tired; all they talked about was wine and prices—this year's crop and last year's—and nobody paid any attention to us children.

My grandmother sometimes told us of her earlier life in that environment. As the only girl among four or five boys, she had learned from her mother how to bake bread, gut fish, skin and dress hares and rabbits, and pluck chickens. She was disappointed that my mother, her oldest daughter, refused to learn those skills, and, to make up for it, she taught me. Of course, in those days we had never heard of tularemia or salmonella, and so she went ahead happily tutoring me how to eviscerate a chicken with my bare hands. "Careful, careful, you must not crush the gallbladder or the meat will taste bitter." Do today's children know where the biblical words "bitter gall" come from? I still have my grandmother's handwritten cookbook. The recipe for the traditional Christmas dinner starts with "First, select a nice male carp ..." How do you know whether a fish is "nice" or, for that matter, "male"? Where do you find a fishmonger today—and if you found one, would he know?

While I was growing up I had no use for my grandmother's instructions. But they came in very handy during World War II. My husband and I were then living in Vermont, and chickens—if you were lucky enough to get one that had already been killed—arrived fully feathered. Thanks to my grandmother, I knew how to string them up on a clothesline, pluck them—a messy job which attracted swarms of black flies—and then singe them over a flame to burn off the remaining pinfeathers.

During one year, when meat was very hard to get, we were the recipients of a winter-long unexpected supply of undressed ducks, quail, rabbits, venison, and fish of all kinds—part of the chase or catch of a famous hunter and fisherman who lived in a nearby village. He wanted to marry my friend Ella Berger from Newfoundland and thought, mistakenly, that I would be swayed by all these presents to influence Ella in his favor. Of course, I never advised her one way or another, but I gratefully accepted whatever the hunter brought to our house. Thanks to my grandmother's tutoring, I was able to convert the gifts into edible meals. (Ella eventually did marry the hunter—in what, she told me later, "must have been a fit of absent-mindedness"; they were soon divorced.)

My grandmother was a quiet woman, unlike the rest of the Lahnsteins, who were an outgoing crowd with a violent temper; their outbursts frightened everybody within hearing. Mostly they fought over money—how to make it, how to save it, or how to spend it—a trait which, alas, obsessed my mother to the end of her days. Every so often their belligerence spun out of control. One sunny Whitsun weekend a harmless family party degenerated into a free-for-all, in the course of which my grandfather, his son, and a son-in-law managed to throw each other down from a balcony. And as soon as one of them landed in the street, he picked himself up, re-entered the house, and began attacking his male relatives all over again. The women screamed, the neighbors called the police, and it became a great scandal. Uncle Albert, the universal problem-solver, had to use all his influence to keep it out of the papers—otherwise, he said, it would be all but impossible ever to find husbands for us girls. No decent man would want to marry into a family of brawlers!

I know nothing of the other grandparents, the Schmitzes, whose genes I inherited as well. They were shadowy people of

whom we had no photos or other mementos. One ancestor report-
edly emigrated to California during the gold rush in the 1850s. It
was a long voyage around the Cape, and nothing was ever heard
from him again. From which my mother concluded that he must
have struck it rich and therefore did not want to get in touch with
the family, with whom he would be obliged to share some of his
wealth. She never believed that he might have died—the ship
might have foundered, he might have succumbed to the terrible
living conditions in the gold fields, he might have been killed in a
bar fight—whatever. The chances for survival were not too good.

Still, when my mother came to the United States for the first
time, in 1954, she wrote to all the Schmitzes in the San Francisco
telephone book and asked them whether they were descendants of
a Schmitz who came over during the gold rush. Some people even
replied, Sorry, no, their great-grandfather was not that Schmitz.

That encompasses the entire family history. There were no stories about my father's childhood. I don't know anything about his
school years or what he did as a young man. Once he took me to
Cologne to visit his parents. I think it was just after the War. That
was the only time I saw them. Being a "Schmitz" in Cologne was almost synonymous with being nobody and everybody. It was the
most common name. If you stood at a street corner and called out,
"Oh, Herr Schmitz, just a moment," a dozen people would answer.
(In Vienna a dozen people come running when you call out "Oh,
Herr Doktor . . .")

THE CHILDREN

O nce my grandfather Lahnstein got over the shock of our arrival, he seemed to grow quite fond of us as long as we were
conveniently kept out of his way and brought out only when he
was in good humor. A self-made man, he was intensely aware of
how little formal education he had; now he tried to compensate by
insisting that we become exemplary students. He gave us coins if
we did sums or spelled right and scolded us when we didn't. German is a fiendishly difficult language to spell. Once I misspelled
the word "Vieh" (cattle), which is pronounced "Fee"; I still remember his reproach: "How could you?"

In retrospect I realize how restricted our life was; at the time we
did not know, of course. My sister and I were even made to sleep in
cribs until we were seven and five years old. There was no reason
for that; we could have slept in beds in our uncle's room while he
was away in the army. We were not allowed to play with the lovely
dollhouse that once belonged to our mother and her sisters and
that was now stored in the attic. "Bring it down? Too much bother.
Besides, the War will be over one of these days. Carl will want his
room back, and you will have to clear out." Because we could never

invite any children to play at the grandparents'—too much noise, too much confusion—we were never asked to play at other children's homes, except once a year at a birthday party for a child of my mother's best friend. On those occasions we brought as a snack a piece of bread and jam from home. The food rations for each household were much too meager to allow hosts to feed their guests.

Apart from these rare occasions or during family visits, we were expected to be happy playing with our dolls with their vacuous eyes. Sometimes in the evening I stood by the window and looked at the flocks of birds flying around in formations. If only I could be one of them and soar above the oppressing environment which appeared to stretch to the rim of the world. Like the rest of the apartment, the space assigned to us was stuffy and overcrowded with things. Framed photographs stood on little tables which were covered with brocade or lace. On the walls hung dark, gloomy paintings or, more likely, copies of paintings by Kaulbach (a favorite painter of the eighties) and of Boecklin's *Island of the Dead*. Over our cribs were Japanese ukiyoe woodcuts featuring long-necked Japanese ladies—souvenirs somebody had brought home from the Vienna Werkstaette.

Germans were—and probably still are—fanatics about fresh air. But we children were not hung out of the windows like the sheets, pillows, and eiderdowns that were aired daily. Instead, we were taken on walks every single day except when it rained heavily. I cannot explain why the Germans had that compulsive fixation on fresh air. It may have had something to do with their collective memory of the stuffiness of the medieval cities. Conditions had been no different in France, England, or the Netherlands. There too, the city walls had enclosed a small space in which narrow-fronted houses were crowded together. Stale air, polluted by human and animal waste, hung on forever. But only the Germans reacted or, shall we say, overreacted once the walls came down. Although they built houses beyond the gates, in the fields and among the trees, they went on capturing fresh air as if it were a vanishing commodity. Even today there are no window screens in Germany. People prefer to have flies and mosquitoes come in through open windows rather than put up screens that, according to popular opinion, keep fresh air out.

During our daily airings we children were as isolated as at the grandparents' apartment. Often we passed by other children who were playing together in the park while their nannies visited among each other. But my mother was not a nanny, and thus we children were excluded from the group. When my mother happened to meet one of her childless friends who was walking her dog, she ordered my sister and me to walk hand-in-hand six steps ahead. When we slowed down, or tried to skip and run, Mrs. X. compared us loudly and unfavorably to her dog, whom she could control with a leash.

$\mathcal{M}$y mother's model for bringing up children was the regimen of the Prussian army. Indeed, she often told us that her secret dream had been to become an elementary school teacher in East Prussia, the very center of a culture which demanded blind obedience and strict discipline. "Why didn't you?" we wanted to know. "Because it would have ruined grandfather's credit," she said. If a well-to-do businessman allowed a daughter to take a paid job, it could only mean that he was near bankruptcy and could not support her. "I did not want to get married so young, either," she continued, "but I had to." Her sister Lisbeth, who was next in the birth order, was a ravishing beauty, full of vitality and imagination; the family was horror-stricken when she declared that she wanted to go on the stage. "Impossible," said Aunt Flora, "why, even the great actress Eleanora Duse 'lost her purity.'" It was obviously imperative to marry Lisbeth off fast. Because of her extraordinarily good looks one could probably find her a rich husband. But according to the then prevailing tradition, Lisbeth could get married only after her older sister, my mother, had been married off. Otherwise people would have talked: "What's wrong with the Lahnsteins? If they can't find a husband for Clara it can only mean that she is suffering from a physical or mental ailment, and, as you know, those things run in the family, and in all likelihood Lisbeth has the same disease ..." Nobody asked whether my mother wanted to get married or even whether she liked Fritz Schmitz. She told us that she saw him for the first time when he came to the Lahnstein's apartment and asked her father for her hand. The family had, of course, made the customary prior enquiries about his character, his business, and his family background, so that it was simply a formality for my grandfather to say yes. It was then decided on the spot that the young couple should go by train to Frankfurt to get the blessing of Aunt Flora and Uncle Albert—the Floberts, as they called themselves. A childless couple, they had appointed themselves protectors of their nieces and nephews and in return demanded to be informed of everything that went on in the family.

At the railroad station Herr Schmitz bought two second-class tickets. My mother's heart sank with foreboding: here it comes. Everybody she knew traveled in third or fourth class; second class was for the rich, and the compartment would probably be empty. Whom could she ask for help if Herr Schmitz forced her to do something which she was really not ready to do? "The train had just passed Hochheim," she said, "when your father took a small box out of his pocket, opened it, and put a ring on my finger. Now we are actually engaged, he said, and I knew I could not get out of that. So, children," she concluded the story, "this is what happens when you travel with a man in a second-class compartment. Promise me that you will never do that."

Frustrated, but still bound by the contemporary mores, she simply transferred her vision of herself as an East Prussian schoolteacher to the Mainz environment, and worked on our education as if we were young army recruits. We were trained to carry out unquestioningly whatever she ordered us to do. She did not allow us to have, let alone express, any opinion on anything, to make even the slightest decision about what to wear, or even to speak up. When an aged great-aunt asked something like "What's the name of your favorite doll?" my mother threw us threatening looks which meant that we were not to answer but let her speak for us. When somebody offered us a cookie, my mother declined: "No, thanks, the children are not hungry." Of course, I was starving hungry, but I would never have dared to speak up and say so.

It was a stultifying life—no spontaneity, no chance to stretch and enlarge one's horizon, no encouragement to explore—only a constant pressure to fit in, to be inconspicuous, and, above all, to do my mother proud: to be the neatest, quietest, and best-behaved child in all of Mainz. Like many people of her generation, she admired the Victorian ambience, or at least its idealization in the media. We were supposed to look and behave like those imagined well-bred English children. My long hair was rolled up in stiff paper curlers every night—I still remember how hard it was to find a sleeping position that did not give me a headache—and combed out into long curls in the morning. Even in summer we wore long-sleeved and high-necked dresses; when other children played in a sandbox, we were made to sit on the sideboards lest sand get on our white batiste dresses.

There was neither TV nor radio; we had a gramophone, but only very few records. Most of the music in our lives came from the small orchestra in the park, from occasional military bands, or from itinerant organ grinders. Whenever one of those fellows appeared for a performance in the street or in a courtyard, he attracted a crowd. Windows opened in nearby houses, and coins rained on the pavement. Organ grinders always traveled with small monkeys that were trained to pick up the coins, drop them into a little hat they carried in their paws, and wave to the public. Musically it was not an event worth remembering, but how eagerly we looked forward to those interludes in our daily lives!

There were movies, but these were, as my mother said disparagingly when her younger sisters went once in a while, "entertainment for the proles," and not worth the time for an educated person. In any event, I do not think there were movies for children.

We did not have much physical exercise either—the kind that stretches one's muscles and improves coordination. Girls were not supposed to exercise anyhow, but, more rationally, all physical exercise was discouraged because it was bound to increase one's appetite at a time when there was so little food. On the few occasions when we were taken swimming in the Rhine, we came home ravenous, and so these excursions were discontinued. In retrospect it was probably a good thing—even then the Rhine was heavily polluted, though it had not yet become the sewer it is today. Nevertheless, there were at the riverbank swimming installations, basically floats with a cutout center section which constituted the "pool." You went into the water upriver and drifted along with the strong current to the other end. There you got out, walked back, and let yourself be carried downstream, over and over again. There was no children's wading basin; with a cork ring tied around our middle, we just went in upstream like everybody else and drifted downstream. I suppose men were able to swim against the current, but we never saw any because there were separate swimming times for men and women. Ten years or so later, a few hours were set aside for "family swimming," but it was a racy young woman who would venture to appear there, certainly not a married woman with or without her children.

The family exposed us early and eagerly to great literature. We were introduced to the poetry and plays of Schiller and Goethe, the famous German classical writers, almost as soon as we came out of diapers. I cannot have been more than five or six years old when I was drilled to recite like an automaton the entire passage of the Easter Parade from Goethe's *Faust* on the occasion of my grandfather's birthday. I have read it several times since then; it is impressive, majestic poetry, but surely inscrutable for a little child.

My mother was devoted to Kleist, a fine writer of the early nineteenth century who is now all but forgotten. One of his short stories, "Michael Kohlhaas," appealed to her especially because it was about a man who ruined himself in the process of fighting "the system"—an endeavor which, I think, my mother wished she had the courage to pursue. I found the book and the subject incomprehensible but didn't dare to say so—after all, it was a "classic." For bedtime stories, my mother read to us during one whole long summer the exploits of the Red Baron von Richthofen, one of Germany's most daring air aces. "Then I was on Frenchie's tail, and with a burst of my trusty machine gun . . ." I cannot for the life of me understand why our mother thought that was appropriate bedtime reading. Were we scared of the violent dogfights, or of the brutal glee of the killer when he hit a target? I cannot say. The stories were about singular bewildering events which I could not connect with anything I knew or felt.

We enjoyed Grimm's fairy tales, although the surrealist adventures of the personae puzzled us occasionally: how did it happen that the big bad wolf did not take bites out of Red Riding Hood and the grandmother before he swallowed them? According to the story, both emerged hale and hearty from their unpleasant confinement in the wolf's belly and immediately fell to consuming cake and wine. But never mind, a rescuer, most likely a prince, always appeared at the last moment, and the evildoers were boiled in oil or consumed by fire. Latterly, child psychologists have "cleansed" the stories of the—to them—shocking cruelties. Too bad: we found it eminently satisfactory that in Grimm's magic kingdom the bad people had it coming to them. As soon as we knew how to read ourselves, we were given the (unabridged) *Odyssey* and *Iliad,* as well as the Nibelung saga, probably for the purpose of keeping us occupied for months with those interminable books. We were supposed to be absorbed by the adventures of the various characters; instead, I found the tales fundamentally depressing. The personae of the various narratives, Zeus or Wotan and their assorted offspring, had absolutely no moral or ethical standards; as gods they ought to have known better. I had no idea that all these narratives were about the myths of early human experience. I read them as straight tales. As such, the Nibelung saga, the theme of Wagner's *Ring* cycle, was a veritable catalog of vices: treachery, duplicity, greed and lust for gold, murder, adultery, drug abuse, incest—you name it. A ten-year-old, especially one like me who was well-protected from the world, was bound to be censorious.

Gruesome as the stories were, they did not scare us; we took them to be part of our European heritage. We grieved for the slain Siegfried and for Prometheus, who was so horribly punished for bringing fire to the human race. Zeus had poor Prometheus shackled to a rock and sent an eagle every day to hack away at his liver. Mysteriously, it would grow back overnight, so that the eagle could start over again on his demolition job. Wasn't that terribly painful? But grieving is not the same as trembling with fear. I do not recall that I was ever frightened even of ghosts or ogres. Nor was I afraid of the dark, as so many children are. Actually, I sympathized and more or less identified with the fellow in one of Grimm's tales who left home and traveled the land to learn what fear was.

The only fear that haunted us was my mother's rage when we did something that displeased her. There was no worse terror. I do not think she realized how much she traumatized us with her tongue-lashing and the punishments which were quite out of proportion for our small misdoings—a spilled glass of milk, a spelling mistake, or a task we failed to complete. Of course, she was under great stress, depending as she did on her parents' financial support, which, she anticipated, she would probably need in the future as well. We children were simply an outlet for the tension that set her on edge. She could not rail against her parents, but she could and did rail against us.

I had been looking forward to my sixth birthday, when I would be ready for school. It was customary in Germany—and still is— for children entering first grade to be sent off with a large paper cone filled with sweets as a solace for the first real separation from home. But my secret hope for such a treat came to naught. My mother decided that I did not have to go to school at all; since she had nothing else to do, she herself would teach me the three R's. And that she did with might and main, pulling me by my long hair when I made a mistake, and drilling me endlessly on the multiplication table at home as well as on our walks. Like all children, I learned to write on a slate board with a piece of chalk; after each session, the slate had to be wiped clean with a little sponge that hung by a string from the frame. Much later, perhaps in the third grade, children were allowed to use a pen and ink to write on paper. The pen, or rather its steel nib, had to be dipped every few moments into an inkpot—a tedious and stain-inducing job. Penmanship was serious business. Children had to copy pages and pages of Gothic-script letters with all those whorls and curlicues until the teacher was satisfied.

To avoid problems with the school board, my mother arranged

with an old friend of hers who ran a private school that I would visit there once a month for a check-up on my progress. It was a most peculiar school; two rooms in the lady's apartment had been made into a study hall where perhaps twenty-five children sat around a long table. Two elderly ladies who were the teaching staff concentrated on the basics. There were no creative activities like drawing or music; no recess because there was no place, indoors or outside, for physical activities or running around. And my occasional visits did not help me to make friends with other children.

What I did enjoy were the daily walks in and around the city. Mainz was an attractive city with an interesting history. Strategically located, it had probably been a settlement before Caesar and his troops arrived to build a bridge across the Rhine. He documented the engineering process in the book *Bellum Gallicum,* which was obligatory reading for every German schoolchild who studied Latin. Having had to spend a whole year on that treatise, I am qualified to say that it is the dullest book ever. Soldiers and engineers rarely are gifted writers. "And then you take this here pylon and mount it on this there beam . . ." It goes on and on and was undoubtedly all true because during our childhood plenty of decayed wood pieces were offered for sale, allegedly remnants of Caesar's bridge, which divers from time to time brought up from the bottom of the river. Who knows? They may have been genuine relics. There were other leftovers, half-ruined fortifications and an aqueduct just out of town. During excavations archaeologists would discover foundations of Roman edifices. The Limes, the old fortified wall which Caesar had built against the Germanic tribes, ran through the wooded hills near Mainz; when we were somewhat older we used to go out by ourselves to dig in the ruins. Sometimes we found Roman coins and shards under stones which had crumbled off the wall. My mother maintained that the broken ceramics came from an old flower pot that she had thrown away some time ago, but we knew better.

The German successors to the Romans built a very handsome Romanesque church to which later pieces of Gothic architecture were added. The impressive cathedral was dedicated to St. Martin. A statue of the saint mounted on a roof of the choir shows him on a horse in the process of giving half his coat to a beggar. This good deed probably did not make him a saint but may have contributed to his eventual sanctification. We, my sister and I, while admiring his charitable conduct, would sometimes speculate what his mother said when he came home with only half of his good coat. We knew what our mother would have said . . .

Next to the cathedral was a statue of Gutenberg, a native of Mainz. It was he who in the fifteenth century invented movable type and enabled the common man to become literate. Before his time there were only handwritten books, laboriously copied and illustrated by monks, which were much too expensive for laypeople to read, let alone to own. "Why is there a statue of Gutenberg?" asked my sister. "Because he is dead," I said. "What did he die of?" "He probably swallowed his baby teeth," I replied. After all, we had been told that this fatal end awaited us if we objected to have our loose baby teeth yanked out. (One end of a piece of thread was fastened to a tooth, the other end to a door handle, and then the door was shut.) It did not occur to me that the man on the pedestal had made it to an age when baby teeth are no longer a problem.

Every once in a while my mother went to visit her father at his store close by the cathedral. I do not know what the visits were about—perhaps about money, perhaps about my grandfather's womanizing, of which I only learned many years later. "You didn't hear about that?" asked my informer. "Everybody in Mainz knew about it. It was said that your grandfather kept a veritable harem, a whorehouse, not a warehouse, in back of his store." It wasn't until then that I understood why everybody referred to my grandmother as "that poor woman." She did not seem to be poor in the sense that the parents of Hansel and Gretel were poor: she had nice clothes and she lived in a nice apartment. Why then did people call her "poor"?

While my mother and grandfather "had words," nobody paid attention to us children. Roaming through the store, we raced the overhead money cages which carried the customers' payments from the sales counters to a central cashier and returned with the change. We prevailed upon the elevator operator to let us ride up and down—customers were allowed only to ride up, but we were the boss's privileged grandchildren. On the top floor we looked in on the advertising department, which consisted of one "artist" whose job was to write figures on price tickets. We admired his work no end—no matter how much we tried, we never managed to draw those florid lines without a stencil. In the children's department, we pretended that we were going to buy dresses for ourselves. Actually, we would never have been allowed to have any of the over-decorated, gaudy off-the-rack clothes. They were for the peasants and the lower classes in the city.

Our clothes and all the clothes of the females in the family were custom-made by a seamstress, usually a poor spinster or a "single" mother, who worked out of her home. We hated having to go for fittings; the stale air in the poor lodgings smelled of last night's supper and of the moldering heaps of cloth. In those depressing quarters we had to stand motionless on a chair, while the seamstress, her mouth full of pins, circled around us on her knees to pin up a hem. After she finished with one child, she began all over with the next one and, after that, with the grown-ups. It was the most tedious procedure, and it was not in the least mitigated by the seamstress's assertion that whatever she was sewing was "the latest chic," as anyone could see from the grimy fashion journals that were lying around.

Fortunately, visits to my grandfather's store or to the seamstress were the exception, not the usual destination of our daily outings. We particularly liked walking on a road that led to the cemetery beyond the city walls. There was almost always a funeral cortege of black-clad men and women following a flower-bedecked coffin. I admired the huge wreaths which the mourners carried, and especially those that were decorated with artificial flowers made of glass beads. They were the most splendid ornaments; it seemed a pity to leave them in the cemetery, where only a few people would see them. Why couldn't we buy one and hang it on the wall in the living room? One day I asked my mother to let us follow the cortege when it entered the cemetery gate. I wanted to find out what was going on in there. "No," said my mother, "we are not going inside. Period." "Oh, well," I retaliated, "when you are dead and in a coffin I can go in, can't I?" Years later my mother told me that she was so shaken by my unequivocal anticipation of her death that she never took us on that particular walk again.

A less controversial walk led along the Rhine river embankment, where we were entertained by the ever-changing sights on the water. There was constant traffic of all kinds of tugs and barges, of boats and ships and rafts, carrying goods down the river and bringing back coal from the Ruhr mines. The Rhine was the most important north-south passage in Western Germany. Roads, such as there were, were unpaved, and most of the small number of trucks that had been built before the War had been commandeered by the army. The boatmen and their families lived on board the ships. We envied the children playing on deck and leading what we thought was a wonderful untrammeled life—no school and no need to live up to the neighbors' standards. We did not think of the women's hard life on board. They had to draw drinking and washing water from the dirty river and keep house in miserable damp and cramped quarters. And probably they were always worried that their children would fall overboard and drown.

We never tired of watching the floats that were made of lashed-together logs. The men in charge of those large timberworks jumped from one round log to another and never lost their balance retrieving strays with long iron hooks and keeping the rudderless frames away from the riverbanks.

I was only three years old when the War broke out, and I did not comprehend what it all meant. Four years older when the War ended, I was deeply affected by the visible signs of the army's defeat—so much so, that it stayed with me as the most dramatic experience in my whole life.

It started with footsteps in the street. One evening when we were already in bed, we heard them, listless shuffling on the cobblestones. They kept on and on till we fell asleep; and when we woke up the next morning they were still there. The War was over; the Mainz bridge across the Rhine was the main return route for the army that had been beaten in France and Belgium. "Like Napoleon's army retreating from Moscow," said my grandfather; he pulled out a picture showing the frozen bodies in the Russian wasteland. "The officers fled in comfort and let the poor guys die," he added, "just like now." Indeed, the officers had commandeered cars, horses, and trains and ran back home ahead of the common soldiers, the cannon fodder. They were the ones who had to slog their way through the rainy and cold November in their dilapidated uniforms and their worn footwear. We stood in the street and watched the seemingly endless rows straggle by. Some years ago I read that the army came back in good order while bands were playing marching songs. But I do not remember hearing any music, only the monotonous footfalls of the sad wretches who were walking along day and night. "Don't they ever sleep?" we asked. Perhaps in empty barns or in a wet field out of town—no one knew. The wounded who were not able to walk were lying in rough wooden carts that were pulled by skeleton-like horses. Their bloodstained bandages were filthy; many of the men had lost arms or legs. Others had only a huge bandaged lump where their head should have been. It was a horrible sight. How those poor men must have suffered on that long weary ride! In the main street the Red Cross handed out coffee, wine, and soup. The soldiers did not stop: they took the mugs and drained them while walking on. We children had to run alongside and bring the empty mugs back. My mother, who had saved a small bottle of brandy from I don't know when, stood with us in the street and looked at the exhausted men. "Here is somebody who can use it," she called all of a sudden, and threw the bottle into one of the open carts. A heavily bandaged soldier caught it, held his hand up for a moment as a kind of salute and smiled. I will never forget that.

The terrible retreat was the first time the horrors of war became real. Anybody who wants to know what that war was like ought to read *All Quiet on the Western Front,* by the German author Erich Maria Remarque, watch the play *Journey's End,* by the Englishman R. C. Sherriff, and see the shattering movie *Oh! What a Lovely War* (directed by Richard Attenborough). In one of that movie's unforgettable scenes, Death in the shape of a skeleton walks among the soldiers in the trenches and hands out a red poppy to those who are destined to be killed in action the next day. Whenever I see a red poppy, so common in Europe, I can't help thinking of the fields of red poppies in Flanders where so many promising young men lost their lives—for what? The end of the War did not end the suffering of the survivors. What would become of those poor foot soldiers? How far would they have to walk beyond Mainz—perhaps through the whole width and breadth of Germany? How could the nation be held to account for the wasted lives, for the wasted bodies, the wasted years?

I am not sure whether the Kaiser was chased away before or after the soldiers came home; but I do remember that my mother took me to the Cathedral Square when his abdication was announced. The people shouted with joy to be rid of their calamitous ruler, and even more deliriously when the hated Crown Prince's abdication was proclaimed immediately after. The Kaiser by then had fled ignominiously into exile in Holland, where he spent the rest of his life, so it was said, sawing wood.

THE FRENCH ARRIVE

𝒯he day after the last of the German troops had passed through, the victors arrived. And what a splendid sight they were! We stood by the window and gazed at the Spahis, the African troops who were part of the French Army. They were well-nourished and handsome horsemen clad in colorful uniforms. They sat well on beautiful black horses and flung bright red capes around like matadors. I do not know what the grown-ups thought—for us it was a fantastic spectacle. We were even more impressed when some of the French soldiers actually appeared at our apartment. We did not know, of course, that they came to requisition our rooms. A man from the mayor's office explained, "I am sorry, Herr Lahnstein, but we have to take over space in your apartment for the occupiers." There was nothing to be done—the French were to be lodged in the best residences all over town. They took the whole flight of rooms going out on the street and left us to arrange ourselves in back as best we could. When they first moved in they tried to make friends. "Hey kids, want some bread?" They held out chunks of snow-white bread we had never seen before, let alone tasted. "We do not eat the enemy's bread," said my mother, and snatched us away.

Soon after the arrival of the French, my father and Uncle Carl came home, both embittered and resentful men who made themselves and the whole family miserable. Everybody was fighting all the time. My father had no business and no job, and neither he nor anybody else knew what his future was going to be. The Lahnsteins held him in contempt because he lacked the qualifications for a businessman: he avoided decision-making, risk-taking, and planning ahead. He would have made an excellent civil servant, somebody who can be relied on to follow orders and execute them faithfully. But there were no openings as the returning soldiers reclaimed their old jobs in a country that had lost a substantial part of its territory under the Treaty of Versailles.

The situation in the Mainz household became so untenable that we had to move out. But where? It so happened that Uncle Albert and Aunt Flora owned a summer place, a house in Koenigstein in the Taunus woods, some thirty miles away from Mainz. That house too had been taken over by the French—much to the chagrin of the owners. They forthwith claimed they urgently needed space to shelter their homeless niece (my mother) and her family. The French agreed to vacate one room, and my mother moved us in, while my father traveled all over Germany to look for a job. The French officers who occupied the house agreed to share the toilet and the washing facilities with us, but not the kitchen, the inner sanctum of all good Frenchmen. For several months we had to eat out in one or the other local restaurant. By and by the French let us have two more rooms, plus the kitchen, and life became more comfortable. However, my mother did not know how to cook, and we still had to go out for our midday meal. We were embarrassed because everybody else's mother knew how to cook, but we could not do anything about that. Nor could we persuade our mother to let us go to the party which the local French commander gave for all the local schoolchildren. My mother declared once again, "We do not eat the enemy's bread." "It isn't bread," we said, "it is cake and ice cream." We did not prevail. All the other children went; my sister and I were kept at home. The French were all over the place; they conducted the Catholic church service in French, and when the priest preached, "Il n'y a qu'un Dieu, et c'est le bon Dieu français" (There is only one God, and He is the Good French God), my mother stormed out.

KOENIGSTEIN

*K*oenigstein was a small town, rather a village, clustered around a hill which was topped by the ruins of an old knights' fortress. Legends, Shakespeare's plays, and perhaps the sight of knights' body armor in museums may have created the myth that all knights were noblemen and noble men. In fact, the garden variety of knights, of whom there were thousands all over Germany, were the original teenage gangbangers. They were in liege to some regional prince and had to obey when he called them to fight under his banner. In the intervals between such excursions they built their own little fiefdoms and engaged in highway robbery. From their hilltop lookouts they swooped down on merchants who traveled the trade routes through the valleys and pillaged, plundered, and killed. Out of boredom they occasionally attacked another gangster on his turf on a nearby hill. All the fortifications were built to withstand attacks; there were moats, drawbridges, and heavy gates. In the walls were slits through which the insiders planned to pour boiling tar on the attackers. And, just in case, there was an escape route: a labyrinth of subterranean passages which led to a camouflaged outlet in the woods at the side of the hill.

The end of medieval feudalism put the surviving knights out of business, the fortress fell into ruins, and the erstwhile serfs who lived at the bottom of the hill turned to farming as a livelihood. By the time we arrived in Koenigstein the population consisted of farmers, tradesmen, and craftsmen such as blacksmiths, saddle-makers, and wheelwrights, and teachers, preachers, and two or three physicians who made house calls by driving one-horse shays. There was a small hospital run by the Sisters of St. Clare, I believe, and a convent run by nuns of the Ursuline order.

A number of wealthy people from Frankfurt and even farther away had discovered the attractions of the wooded undulating hills and the refreshing air of the Taunus ridges. The Frankfurt Rothschilds, the Grand Duchess of Luxemburg, and the chairman of an important industrial conglomerate were among the first to build elaborate estates there, where they spent several months each year. They arrived in their equipages, followed by a train of vehicles filled with all the paraphernalia considered necessary for a stay in the country. A little later a railway line was built to con-nect Koenigstein with the industrial city of Hoechst at about the midpoint between Frankfurt and Mainz. The narrow-gauge little train stopped for passengers at each of the six small villages be-tween the two terminals and took some forty minutes to cover the twelve-mile distance. The availability of railway transportation in-duced a fair number of other well-to-do families to build second homes, though on a less opulent scale. The natives began to cater to these semi-permanent visitors and to the even more numerous transient summer guests. They transformed their houses into "Pensions" or spruced up rooms for rent. They set up a couple of coffee shops and other amenities and even built a swimming pool in a nearby valley, although a strong minority in the planning com-mission objected that there was no need for it. "Let people climb into their rain barrels if they want to get wet."

But what really put Koenigstein on the map were two world-renowned sanatoriums. In the early 1900s, a sanatorium was what a health farm is now: a place to get a massage. The only difference is that at a health farm the massage is for the body, whereas the sanatorium massage was, or still is, for the ego. Were you a bored housewife who needed a change? A woman who suffered from depression because her husband had threatened to shoot her lover? An artist whose creative juices had dried up? Whatever your real or imagined problems, off you went for a stay at a sanatorium for as long as you could pay the very steep costs.

Many of the patients were celebrities, conductors, actors, or writers—people like Alexander Moissi, the Albanian-Italian actor who was to play the title role of *Everyman* in Salzburg, the music conductor Otto Klemperer, and many others who were famous then or became famous much later. The painter Ernst Ludwig Kirchner was a longtime patient at the Sanatorium Kohnstamm; being short of funds he suggested that as payment for the expensive treatment he would paint frescoes around the walls of the dining room. Alas, in the thirties the Nazis classified his art as "degenerate" and had the walls indelibly painted over. Kirchner also painted a portrait of Dr. Kohnstamm, the sanatorium's founder and director, which he presented to the doctor's wife. Unfortunately, Mrs. Kohnstamm did not like the painting at all; she thought her husband was much better looking in real life. After Kirchner left the sanatorium she cut the picture into little pieces and threw it into the trash. Considering the prices which Kirchner's paintings fetch today, that was a million-dollar mistake.

There was a kind of decadent aura around the sanatoriums, with their large, flower-filled common rooms. Outside there were rows upon rows of deck chairs for the patients to lie on. I could not explain why it all seemed so unhealthy. It was not until I read Thomas Mann's *Magic Mountain* years later that I understood the many facets of invalidism.

In our tight living quarters home schooling was no longer an option, and shortly after we came to Koenigstein my sister and I were enrolled in a regular public school. For most children it is a traumatic experience to move to a new locality where they are the new kids on the block. For us it was a liberation from the Mainz constraints, and we found it an exhilarating change for the better. Our mother, however, must have had a miserable and lonely time. She had so many strikes against her: a married woman whose husband was hardly ever on the scene. And she was a foreigner—the natives considered everybody who was not born and raised in the village to be a foreigner. Nor could she be assigned a place in any of the separate layers which defined the social structure in the community.

$\mathcal{B}$efore the War, merchants and businessmen and, worst of all, retailers like the Lahnsteins, were at the bottom of the heap, slightly above small tradesmen or journalists and slightly below manufacturers and bankers. In the next higher rank were the professionals—lawyers, doctors, pharmacists, and the lower levels of the civil service. Above those were the academicians, the Herr Professors, of superior status compared to those below, but inferior, far inferior to the Officer Corps. People who were born into one layer of society stayed there and did not mix with other strata. Even during the annual carnival, when the usual social boundaries were suspended, a transgression could have serious consequences. Before the War—during the War there was no carnival, of course— Uncle Carl had once gone to a costume ball dressed up as a coquetting girl. In that disguise he flirted with a couple of officers who took him (believing he was a "she") on their laps and treated him to champagne. At midnight the masks came off, and the officers discovered that they had been fooled. They were furious. They said it was an affair of honor and Carl would have to give satisfaction in a duel. "Give me your card, and you'll hear from my adjutant." But when they took a look at Carl's card the officers turned purple: as a merchant's son his status was so low that it disqualified him as a dueling opponent. A disgusting affair: all they could do was to turn their backs on him.

No civilian's child was ever invited to a birthday party given by an army officer's child. True, there were a few opportunities for moving up the ladder: a good-looking daughter of a very rich businessman could hope to marry into the officer's class, or a successful munitions maker like Krupp could rise into the sublime sphere surrounding the Kaiser. But these were exceptions. The caste system was so pervasive that, for instance, my father would not dream of sitting down at a Stammtisch—the table permanently reserved in a tavern or coffeehouse at which men met after work—that was by unwritten consent the domain of the local professionals. His place was at the Stammtisch for businessmen. Aunt Flora was in seventh heaven when she was asked to join the board of some charitable institution; now she could rub shoulders with an honest-to-goodness Frau Professor who was also on the board. Her envious sisters-in-law suspected that she had pulled a lot of strings to finagle that invitation.

The rigid stratification had become somewhat relaxed in the wake of the War, but Koenigstein was behind the times and still insisted that people stay in their predestined place. There were, of course, oddballs, just as there are in other small towns; one family, besotted by Wagner's *Ring* cycle, had named their numerous children after the opera's larger-than-life heroes. Mrs. L. would lean out of the window and shout to her eight-year-old son: "Siegfried, Siegfried, hurry up and put Bruenhilde on the potty!" and similar commands surely not found in the original libretto. But these eccentrics chose isolation by their own free will, and to the world at large they seemed to be happy with it.

My mother's solitude was not by choice. Come to think of it, during our nine years in Koenigstein her only contacts were with people whose social status had slipped. One of them was a physician's family who kept their mongoloid child at home instead of institutionalizing him. The visibility of the disoriented boy tarnished the standing of the family and hurt the father's reputation. People said, "What kind of a doctor is he if he cannot even heal his own son?" Mrs. S. was probably glad to have the company of my unprejudiced mother. Under other circumstances I doubt that she would have been so ready to associate with us.

There was also the widow of the late Dr. Kohnstamm, the sanatorium's founder. Upon the death of her husband she had been demoted, so to speak, in the pecking order. She accepted my mother as one of the few educated (*gebildete*) women in the neighborhood; she even invited her to join the book club, whose members voted on, and jointly purchased, new books which had been favorably reviewed in the Frankfurt newspapers. The books were circulated among the members according to their seniority. As the newest member, my mother was last on the list—a good thing, too. She liked to read in bed, and whenever she came to an exciting passage she brought the book so close to the candle that she singed the page—sometimes several pages at a time. We owned many books in which a reader had to reconstruct entire sections that had been charred beyond recognition.

We children were readily accepted within the community. We played with the children of the local lawyer or physician, with the judge's son or the chemical engineer's daughters. But none of our playmates' parents ever came to our house, nor did they invite our parents to theirs, except once—the evening before we moved away from Koenigstein. An invitation to supper at that time did not disgrace our hosts. We would be gone for good.

My mother did not complain, but I knew she was being snubbed. One distressing incident is imprinted upon my memory. In the early 1920s women still wore their hair long, and every woman who could possibly afford it went to the barber's for a shampoo and set. Without running hot water or a showerhead, the only way to wash one's hair at home was in a cold-water sink. The shop of the Koenigstein barber, or coiffeur as he preferred to be called, was at a crossroads at the very center of the village. Whenever anything exciting happened, it would have to be at that location. One day two hay wagons collided there with a loud crash. The barber ran out of his shop, twirling a curling iron that he had just been using on one of his customers. Behind him came half a dozen ladies in various stages of beautification who were also curious to see what had happened. Draped in white smocks, and with their hair sculpted by white shampoo, they looked like a gaggle of geese lined up behind the gander-coiffeur. Except for my mother, whom the group left standing by herself, like Hans Christian Andersen's ugly duckling. I felt really sorry for her.

I do not know how she managed to fill her days. We had a daily maid, and housekeeping for the three of us wasn't that big a chore anyway. In a fluid society like that of the United States, a new-comer can find a niche by volunteering or joining an interest group, be it watercolor painting or bird watching or something of that nature. In Germany, even today, volunteer work requires licenses, background checks, exams to be passed, investigations, and a frustrating fight with the stakeholders. My mother had no aptitude for sewing or quilting or other traditional time-consuming occupations. There were no concerts or theaters; about the only way for her to pass the time was to read.

Once a week she marched us off in the afternoon to one of the two coffeehouses on Koenigstein's "Main Street" where she spent a couple of hours going through a week of the Frankfurt newspapers which the owner kept on a stacked file. We were embarrassed because no other mother took her children there; everybody passing by in the street could see us through the large glass windows. My mother ordered a cup of coffee for herself and a "Schillerlocke" for us to keep us quiet while she read. A Schillerlocke was a curly pastry cone filled with whipped cream; the name alluded to the eighteenth-century poet Schiller and his bewigged locks. A great many things in Germany alluded to Kultur.

We realized that our mother could not afford to subscribe to the daily Frankfurt paper. But why couldn't she be satisfied "like every-body else" with the local paper, the *Taunus Messenger,* which came out twice a week? It reported all the births, marriage banns, and deaths. It described the accidents of which there were many, as in all rural communities. Children fell off or under a hay wagon; they fell into a well and drowned; they were kicked in the head by a horse; and newborn babies were found dead in the village pond. Sometimes a girl was "surprised by the stork." "Fraulein Maria

Somebody, daughter of the farmer Adam Somebody and his spouse Hilda née Otherbody, was waiting for a train at the Kelkstein railway platform when she was surprised by the stork. Fraulein Somebody was on her way to visit her aunt in Kleinkroetzen." Having read a number of such stories, my sister and I began to watch for a stork whenever we stood on a railway platform. We did not really expect that the bird would drop a baby on us—we were only children. Maybe when we got to be in our teens.

Notwithstanding such interesting stories, our mother was not impressed with the *Taunus Messenger* or, for that matter, with the Important Information which was entrusted to the Town Crier for distribution throughout the village. So the weekly excursions to the coffeehouse continued, and while we enjoyed the pastry treat, we just wished that it would be offered less conspicuously.

Our mother and we children had barely adjusted—or pretended to have done so—to a life that was so different from the Mainz environment, when I came down with what today would probably be diagnosed as mononucleosis. In Koenigstein, and even in Mainz, where mother consulted a physician, it was called glandular fever. I was kept in bed for six weeks. It was a dreary time; there was no public library nor a bookstore. We did not know people well enough at that time to borrow books, and all I had for reading matter was what the Floberts' had left behind: two volumes on the German administration of South West Africa, a former German colony, and a collection of saccharine, pious stories "for ethical-minded girls." Good deeds were always rewarded, though sometimes only posthumously, and terrible punishments were meted out to disobedient children. One story which made a great impression on me was about a child who wanted to play instead of going to church on Sundays. The church bell pealed to remind her, but the stubborn child ran off into the fields. The bell climbed down from the steeple, raced after the girl and jumped on top of her. The poor little thing was trapped inside the metal shell, with the clapper clapping away and making an ear-splitting noise. I do not remember how long the bell sat on top of its prey—didn't it have anything better to do? After a while the child pleaded for mercy and was let out on condition that from now on, etc.

The accumulated moral messages of all these stories may have improved my soul, but they did nothing for my health, which caused some concern in the family. At that stage my mother's sister Lisbeth came up with a brilliant suggestion. "Let Doris come with us to spend the winter in St. Moritz in Switzerland. The mountain air and the sun certainly will be better for her than the cold gray climate in wintry Koenigstein. She can join us in the train when we pass through Mainz on our way to Switzerland."

I did not know Aunt Lisbeth at all; I had never met her. Shortly after my mother became Frau Fritz Schmitz, Lisbeth had married a wealthy Argentinean. Immediately after the wedding her new husband brought her to Buenos Aires on a sea voyage which took three weeks by the fastest ship. Far away in exotic Argentina, and leading an unimaginably glamorous life as the beautiful wife of a wealthy husband, Aunt Lisbeth had been transformed into a veritable fairy-tale princess, at least in the eyes of the Mainz family. As for her husband, his business acumen showed him up as a symbol of wisdom.

The family was thrilled by Aunt Lisbeth's invitation. "That is a rare privilege," they said, and "you don't know how lucky you are." Of course, they were right, but I was panic-struck by the idea of being with total strangers for two or three months. And particularly with strangers who were so rich, beautiful, compassionate, and intelligent—I could not possibly measure up to their standards. Would I remember all the exhortations my mother poured into me day after day?

One evening I was taken to the Mainz railroad station where the express train from Holland came to a breathy halt. A lady reached out from a first-class—first class!—compartment, scooped me up, assured my mother that she would take good care of me, kissed everybody, and then the guard blew his whistle, and the train took off. I cried all night, shaken up by the finality of my departure and scared of the days ahead. By the time we arrived in Switzerland the next morning, I had finally calmed down sufficiently to look at all the members of our traveling group: Aunt Lisbeth, her husband Sigi, their three young children, the children's governess, the baby's nanny, and my aunt's personal maid who, however, traveled third class. The plan was for us to stay in Zurich for a few days to get acclimated before going on to St. Moritz, which is at an altitude of some 6,000 feet. Getting used to the physical elevation was no problem for me. Getting used to the free and easy life style of my hosts was another matter. I reveled in the earthly delights: the beauty of the sunny mountain peaks at noon and the pink afterglow on the snow as the sun withdrew in the evening; the blue ice of the glaciers; the sleigh rides through silent woods to a snowbound village; or the pungency of wood smoke rising from the chimneys and mingling with the scent of thawing snow dripping from housetops in the midday sun.

Impressed though I was at first by the unexpected luxuries which the others took for granted, I quickly and gratefully accepted them without guilt feelings: hot running water which enabled one to have a warm bath at any time; jam AND butter—not one or the other—on a piece of bread; or the custom-made figure skating boots which my aunt ordered from the best store in St. Moritz. Before we went skiing, Aunt Lisbeth phoned the hotel ski shop, and by the time we came downstairs a valet was waiting for us with our skis, waxed for the day's snow conditions. At the skating rink we sat down on a bench, while kneeling attendants took our shoes off and laced up the skating boots. I doubt that this kind of service exists anywhere today.

I knew that money could buy all these splendid things, and that neither I nor anybody in the family back in Germany could ever hope to be as rich as the relatives from Argentina. But there was something else my uncle and my aunt had which was not tied to money: freedom from small anxieties, fears, and prejudice.

On one of the first days in St. Moritz, Uncle Sigi invited me to go sledding with him and one of his children, down the long hill from our hotel to the village at the bottom. At the end of the run we would take the cog railway back up the hill. He and little Paul got on one sled, I on another, and we took off. Since they were so much heavier they got to the bottom ahead of me. By the time I arrived they were gone. I could not find them; I was abandoned! What was I to do? I had no money for the railway fare, and it was much too long a walk to climb up on foot. I just stood there and cried. Soon some strangers offered help and advice. "Why don't you just ride up—you'll meet your uncle at the top, to be sure." "Impossible," I said. I had seen people ejected from streetcars in Mainz if they had no money for the fare. "Don't worry," said the good Samaritans, "we'll explain it to the conductor." So they did and, incredibly, he let me ride up for free. I worried about what Uncle Sigi would say. My mother would have spanked me for having caused her anxiety. Aunt Lisbeth and Uncle Sigi did not believe in spanking, but there were worse punishments: perhaps they would send me back home as an irresponsible kid? Nothing of the sort: my uncle was waiting for me at the top. "Oh, there you are! We were looking for you, but when we did not see you we thought you might have come up before us. You were not worried, were you? No, I don't think you would be. Now, let's go in." I did not walk, I floated on air. He had told me in so many words that he trusted me to handle a difficult situation. He gave me a self-confidence which I never had before. It was a heady feeling.

Inevitably the glorious days came to an end; my health was completely restored. Although I had been dutifully looking forward to being again with my own family, I was distraught at the idea of leaving my cheerful relatives in St. Moritz. Aunt Lisbeth promised that she would invite me again next winter, but that was nine months away, an eternity.

While I was away, things at home had taken a turn for the better. My father had found a good job in Frankfurt as a sales manager, and my mother had been "surprised by the stork" at the hospital—certainly a much more convenient drop-off place than a railroad platform. We now had a brand-new baby brother—and a mother who had become extraordinarily relaxed. My sister and I agreed that this drastic change was a real miracle. A year or so earlier, when we had been hospitalized for scarlet fever, we had become so fond of the Sisters who ran the hospital with so much loving care that we prayed for one of the nuns to become our mother or, if that was not possible, that our mother would become a kindhearted nun. It seemed that our mother's visit to the hospital really had worked wonders. She said that she had not expected to have a third child, and she kept referring to the baby as "my little mistake"; nevertheless, her maternal love, which had been suppressed for so long by her insecurity (and the compensatory need to present herself as a domineering authority), emerged from wherever she had kept it hidden and enveloped not only the baby but us older children as well. We were not used to all that affection and basked happily in the good feeling.

My grandmother was at the time in a nursing home about an hour away from Koenigstein. On our weekly visits to her bedside we had to walk through the woods on a trail on which ants had established a major crossroad for the colony. Thousands and thousands of ants ran back and forth between a tall anthill at one side and whatever they were doing on the other side of the trail. The moment one put a foot down into that busy swarm, dozens of ants started to crawl up one's shoes, socks, bare legs, and beyond. "I hate ants," I said, "I don't want to step across." "Come on," said my mother; she picked me up and set me down at the other side of the crawlers. I was so relieved, I fell around her neck saying "thank you, thank you." "That was easy, wasn't it?" she said. "I hope I can always carry you that easily over whatever difficulties will be in your future path." I shall always remember that unique testimony of tenderness. My mother did not allow herself to be so affectionate again face-to-face until she was in her seventies.

I admit that I was not terribly interested in the new baby brother—according to the then prevailing dogma, all older siblings were germ carriers and had to be kept away from a new baby. We were not allowed to help feed him or carry him around, and so I did not develop a sense of attachment. It was far more rewarding to play with dolls and, especially, to rekindle with and through them the glorious days of St. Moritz before they faded from my memory.

Actually, it turned out to be an interesting year. The Floberts and Frau Hausmann, Aunt Flora's aged mother, came to stay for the summer in what was, after all, their house. We were relegated to rather cramped quarters on the top floor, but as the old lady's favorite companion I spent most of my time downstairs anyhow. During our school vacations I sat with her, morning after morning, on the large veranda which encircled the house, and read to her or listened to her stories. Born around 1840, she had married a railway engineer, who brought his young bride to the United States, where he had a job overseeing the construction of one of the transcontinental railroads. The young couple liked America and life beyond the narrow horizon of provincial Germany. In due course they became American citizens. Mrs. Hausmann accompanied her husband on most of his travels; once, she told me, they came to a place where Abraham Lincoln was giving a speech. "He was the homeliest man you ever saw," she said, "but the moment he started to speak you forgot his looks and everything else." I knew nothing about Lincoln or, for that matter, about America, except that it was a place where some people went to make their fortune and to which others were sent as punishment for their misdeeds. To redress my ignorance Mrs. Hausmann made me read *Uncle Tom's Cabin,* in the German translation of course. I appreciated her concern, and I was moved by the suffering of Uncle Tom and all his pitiable fellow slaves. But I did not understand the book at all. Sure, the ancient Greeks and Romans took their vanquished foes home as slaves—but that was hundreds of years ago. It was inconceivable that slavery really existed in Mrs. Hausmann's lifetime. I tried, as best I could, to get her to switch to less distressing stories and talk about the wilderness in which she lived with her husband and their three little children. Eventually, the family had returned to Germany so that the children could get a proper education.

We had been so used to living in a fatherless household that we did not quite know what to expect if our father were to assume the role of a breadwinner and head of the family. But that was not going to happen in the immediate future. Koenigstein was in the zone that was occupied by the French, but my father's job was in Frankfurt, which was not occupied. The French, as well as the Germans, made it as difficult as possible to cross from one zone to the other. There was endless harassment at the checkpoints; travel permits issued yesterday were declared invalid today. Sometimes the border was closed altogether for an indeterminate period. In his new job my father could not risk being stuck in the Occupied Zone, and so he had to live apart from us in a rented room in Frankfurt. Some Sundays we got together at a stretch of the border which ran along a ditch in the woods. He, arriving from Frankfurt, sat down on one side of the ditch; we, coming from Koenigstein, sat on the other. We passed food back and forth, careful to keep a distance between us when the mounted border patrol came along. They rummaged through our picnic baskets, inspected our papers, and advised us to "break it up"; another troop might come along and not take as benevolent an attitude of our illicit meeting.

This was one of the more harmless political adventures during the years when the fabric of the German post-War government was fraying all over.

The Treaty of Versailles, which ratified Germany's defeat in World War I, set off anger and frustration throughout the nation. The Weimar government, successor to the Kaiser Reich, was very unpopular, and rabble-rousers attempted to overthrow it by force. We children realized that Germany was in desperate straits when the unstable political conditions produced a rampant inflation. The mark, the unit of currency, kept losing its value. At the beginning of the inflation 4.20 marks bought one dollar; the next month it cost 40 marks to buy one dollar, and from then on the torrent of the mark's depreciation ran wild. The mint could hardly keep up printing bills of larger and larger denominations which were already worthless the day after they were put in circulation. Million-mark bills were pieces of white paper that were printed on one side only. A week after they had been issued, they were no longer worth anything; we used them as scribble paper in school—it would have been more expensive to buy notepads at the stationery store. My mother went to Frankfurt the morning of the day when my father's salary was due, so that she could run quickly to a store and convert the amount into goods: socks, flour, soap—whatever was available. A few hours later the same amount would have lost three-quarters of its value. During that overheated inflation German money was no longer a means of exchange. Prices were quoted in dollars. A farmer who delivered a year's supply of potatoes for our root cellar demanded a fortune, one whole dollar for the wagonload. If you did not have foreign currency you had to pay in tangibles. A piano lesson cost a quarter pound of butter, payable in kind. But the farmers whose cows produced the butter did not want piano lessons—they wanted the pianos, even though they did not know how to play them. Steinway grand pianos were the biggest status symbols. Some country people were said to have not just one but two Steinways, back to back in their poor cottages. Meanwhile, everything the middle class had saved was wiped out. Uncle Albert was in despair; he flailed hopelessly against the monster that was devouring his retirement funds. "When the mark sinks to two billions against the dollar, it will be taps for Germany," he proclaimed. Events proved him right in the end. When the mark was finally stabilized, he had lost everything he owned; he had to go back to work at age sixty-five. Nearly everybody we knew was traumatized as well as impoverished by the catastrophic inflation.

The inflation, in turn, engendered more bitterness and unrest, especially in the Rhineland where the French, for their own political reasons, supported a rowdy group of German "separatists." They were demagogues who agitated for a separate buffer zone between France and Germany, to be carved out from what was unquestionably German territory. Not unreasonably the German majority opposed the idea, but having no guns they were at a disadvantage. One day my mother went to Frankfurt to stay overnight with a cousin. We children and Kaethchen, our maid, were at home when the telephone rang. The father of one of our school friends asked to speak to Kaethchen. The separatists had occupied Koenigstein during the night, he told her. There would be no school today, and she must keep us inside the house. Sure enough, shooting started almost immediately after he hung up. The sound of breaking glass and the thuds of objects being thrown down from housetops made us scurry for safety under the heavy dining table. There we felt quite safe; in fact, we shivered pleasurably as witnesses of so exciting an event. I do not remember how long the separatists hung around, perhaps a couple of days. When it was over we went to look at the damage. Among other things, the vandals had smashed the entire fine china service of the Grand Duchess of Luxemburg, which was stored in the City Hall when she was not in residence.

We got off lightly compared to the havoc the hoodlums wrought elsewhere. But angry opponents finally started to counter-attack by blowing up the railway trains which were run under French supervision. Trying to stop that sabotage, the French in turn demanded that a member of the German Railway Administration ride in the cab of every train, right next to the engineer. For many months, one of Aunt Flora's cousins was one of those unfortunate hostages.

After a while the situation returned to normal, the attacks stopped, and people began to feel sufficiently secure to resume railroad travel. Around that time my mother decided that my sister and I should go to Mainz once a week to take piano lessons. Our minimal proficiency and our total lack of interest certainly did not justify going to such lengths; the real purpose of those trips was for us to go and cheer up our grandfather, who was lonely after my grandmother's recent death. On the appointed day we walked from our house to the Koenigstein railway station and took the train to its end station. There we had to go to another platform for the train to Kastell, a small town that was situated opposite Mainz, on the other side of the Rhine. We walked across a bridge to Mainz and to the piano teacher's house. After our lessons we went to my grandfather's, who treated us to cake and chocolate milk. And then we headed back to Koenigstein the same complicated way. In the trains we always traveled fourth class (which does not exist anymore). Before World War II a fourth-class compartment was a rather large square chamber with a door and a window on opposite sides. The travelers sat on benches around the perimeter of the compartment. Peasants stacked whatever they were taking to mar-

ket in the large empty space in the center: potato sacks, tubs of butter, cages full of chickens, piglets, or rabbits, and often also baby
lambs or goat kids tied to strings. The smell and the animal noises
were high, but the fare for this kind of transportation was also conspicuously low.

The weekly excursions would have gone on for years if our piano teacher had kept her offensive and obscene remarks to herself
instead of lavishing them on us. I said that I was not going to continue and take lessons from that vulgarian. My mother thought
that I was overly critical, but eventually she transferred us to another piano teacher. Not that we made more progress under him.
He was a seventeen-year-old wunderkind, a budding concert pianist whose mother dressed him in short pants to make him appear younger. He annoyed us no end by insisting that we, about
four years his juniors, should address him by the formal "Sie." Like
the rest of the Koenigstein youths we mocked him; and since he
did not know how to deal with snappish thirteen-year-old girls, we
parted company by mutual agreement. Our next piano teacher was
a spinster lady in Frankfurt who, in her youth, had been a student
of Clara Schumann, the famous pianist who, in addition to having
been married to Robert Schumann, was a close friend of Brahms.
Miss W. may not have been an outstanding pianist, in spite of
her background, but she was a good teacher, and I made some
progress—sufficient to be accepted as a pupil at the Frankfurt Conservatory during my senior year in high school. But once I left
Frankfurt I had little opportunity to continue, or, rather, I did not
make the necessary effort, and whatever I had learned up to then
simply vanished.

Our grandfather, who was clearly disappointed at the discontin-
uance of our weekly visits, suggested, no, really commanded, that
henceforth we must spend our school vacations with him in
Mainz. The days were rather dull: we rode around on our bicycles
and entertained ourselves as well as we could while he was at
work. However, every evening he took us to the opera. There was
nothing pretentious about it—people went to the opera then as casually as they go to the movies nowadays. The Municipal Theater
in Mainz, next door to my grandfather's department store, had a

huge repertory and put on a different play or opera every night. It was not always a stellar performance, but it was a marvelous experience for us. In the course of those visits I must have heard practically every opera at least once: all of Mozart, all of Verdi, *Der Freischuetz, Turandot, Carmen, Czar and Carpenter, Louise, Lohengrin, Tannhaeuser, Die Fledermaus, Fidelio, La Traviata, The Barber of Seville,* and many more. Some were musically way above our heads, but no matter. We early understood that opera is really the reproduction of a complicated fairy tale and can be enjoyed on different levels: the music, the libretto, the dance, and the interaction between all three.

I think it was in 1926 that my grandfather bought a car—the first car in the entire family, and that was more or less the end of our frequent visits in Mainz. Instead of having us come to Mainz, he came now Sundays to visit us in Koenigstein. His son, Uncle Carl, had passed the driver's test and was a certified "Gentleman Driver." Originally the term connoted a sporty type, a member of the aristocracy or the upper bourgeoisie—somebody who was not afraid of the new machines and of the risks to which he exposed himself, his passengers, and the people and the animals on, or even off, the roads he traveled. In the post-War days the word was no longer reserved for the upper class, and venturesome young men like my uncle relished the freedom of driving a car without a chauffeur. Besides, earning the right to drive a car was no small accomplishment: a candidate for the test was presented with a disassembled engine—bolts, washers, valve stems, and dozens of other parts—from which he was required to reconstruct a functioning automobile. Only then was he taken outside to learn how to drive. The requirement was not as ridiculous as it seems to us now. Gas stations and repair garages were few and far between. It was a good idea for the operator of a car to know where each replacement had to go. However, my grandfather hired a chauffeur because he did not trust his son to drive. After Sunday lunch and during our grandfather's nap, that good-natured man offered to take us children for a spin around the block. Just us children—it took our breath away. Seeing us in the big car immediately brought out the neighborhood children. That was the time for them to cash in on past favors: "Doris, I am you best friend, am I not? Can I ride with you? Remember, I let you have a bite from my sandwich when you forgot to bring yours . . ." "Of course, of course." We were generous and let everybody crowd in until our grandfather woke up and reclaimed the car for the return to Mainz.

$\mathcal{D}$uring the three months in Switzerland I had not thought about school at all. I assumed that when I was back I might have to make up some of the subjects I had missed. It turned out that was no problem, not because I was particularly intelligent but because the school was so bad. The Taunus Realschule to which we went was considered to be superior to the Volksschule—the local elementary school—because it went beyond the mandatory seven grades and because the curriculum included French and English. It was the only "quality" public school in the vicinity and had such a high reputation that parents in faraway villages sent their children there. For some of those youngsters it meant a six-mile round trip on foot every day, rain or shine.

Actually, the school's educational and pedagogic standards were abysmal. The teachers were uninspiring products of some Normal School who neither knew what they were supposed to teach nor how to. We had to repeat mindlessly and by rote page after page in the textbook, whether it was arithmetic or geography or history. We had to learn and recite by heart the birth and death dates, and the cognomens, of all the emperors of the Holy Roman Empire from Charlemagne on: Philip the Fat, Peg-legged August the Twenty-seventh, Otto the Kinky-Haired One, Ludwig the Dumb One—all right, I am making this up, but only just a little. We did not learn—and of course our teachers did not know either—the role of the various emperors in the history of Europe, why they fought anybody, especially the popes, why Sicily—of all places—suddenly appeared as a province of Austria, what the Children's Crusade had to do with the Knights of Malta, and so forth and so on. In "English language" class a teacher, reading us a sentence, pronounced "butcher" as "but-cher." A British boy in my class whose father was with the British Occupation Army raised his hand. "Excuse me, sir, but in England it is pronounced 'bootcher'." The teacher slammed his hand on his desk. "I don't care how you pronounce it in England; here you pronounce it the way I tell you."

There was no sports program, no arts program, no music. The "gym" was a dirt-strewn, stony school yard with a pair of parallel bars and a trapeze. During the unsupervised recess periods we did acrobatics on that rickety equipment, without even a floor mat to cushion a fall. If one bloodied one's head or arms or legs, one just went in to the sink and washed it off. The teachers were not the least bit concerned.

The only interesting class was religion, which was taught not in Sunday school but in the public schools, by Roman Catholic and Protestant clergymen. Attendance was compulsory except for avowed atheists. My parents were non-religious; they were not atheists, but they were not believers either. When my sister and I were quite small, our mother had taught us the Lord's Prayer in French, as she had learned it in a finishing school in the French-speaking part of Switzerland: "Notre Père qui êtes aux cieux, que votre nom soit sanctifié . . ." Apparently she thought that was sufficient for our religious education. Although the Lahnsteins were ethnically Jewish, they seemed to have no connection with the positive aspects of Judaism. Like many German non-Jewish Jews, they intermarried, they celebrated Christmas, not Hanukah, and Easter but not Passover. Orthodox Jews did not consider them to be Jewish; they asked them to come to their houses on the Sabbath to turn lights on or off—something that they themselves were forbidden to do according to the Jewish ritual. My grandmother went to a temple once or twice a year; my grandfather, who was a freemason, never accompanied her. My mother went to a denominational religious service only on special occasions, or to accompany a friend. She considered herself to be a child of the Enlightenment; she was guided by the words of the philosopher Immanuel Kant: "The starry heavens above me and the moral law within me." This was all that anyone needed. There was no rational proof that God existed. Formal religion was desirable for children and the lower classes, whose sense of rationality was underdeveloped. Servants were encouraged to go to church because that is where they learned honesty and obeisance to their masters. My mother did not care one way or another to which denominational class we went. My father, as usual, had no opinion or, if he had one, he did not voice it. The population of Koenigstein was split almost evenly between Roman Catholics and Lutheran Protestants, plus half a dozen Jewish families. We chose the Lutheran class because of the charismatic teacher.

The Lutheran pastor, Court Preacher B. (the "Court" prefix related to the Grand Duchess of Luxemburg's summer residence), was a tall man with an impressive bearing and a natural gift for storytelling. The Bible came alive in terms we could understand. What did Isaac think when his father took him through the woods to be sacrificed? What would you have thought if you had been in his place? Would you have asked your father why he was so sorrowful? Abraham and Isaac lived in the Judaean Desert; it is unlikely that they walked through woods. But we lived in the woods, we understood the closed-in feeling between the trees and the forlorn sound of twigs when you stepped on them. These were tales of real events which could happen again here and now. "Watch out," said the preacher, "the Good and the Evil are forever fighting for your soul. You may not always recognize the Devil. One of these days he will be coming down the highway from Limburg and you will think, oh, well, he's just like anybody else, but when you look down you will see he has a cloven foot."

For months I looked inquisitively at the trouser legs of the people who traveled that straight steep road which led from the barren crest of the Taunus ridges down to verdant Koenigstein. Mostly the travelers were workingmen from the desolate villages beyond the hills. Day after day, six days a week, they rode on their bicycles to the railroad station to go by train to Hoechst and their jobs in one of the huge chemical factories. At night—there was no eight-hour day—after dark, the exhausted men had to push their bicycles the five miles uphill to get home. They could not make a living as farmers—there was not enough arable land where they lived. The soil was too poor and the climate too raw. Hoechst was the nearest place for steady employment. It was a wretched way of living— and it seemed unlikely that the Prince of Darkness would assume the persona of one of those desperately poor men.

I was not so sure that Satan was not hiding among the gypsies who also came traveling down the same highway but, of course, not every day. Most Americans probably have never seen gypsies— except perhaps as tourist attractions in the French Camargue or in Spain. Before Hitler declared them an inferior race, to be deported and killed in concentration camps, gypsies were nomads who roamed all over Europe. They had their own rites and traditions, and they married only within the tribe. They never settled down for an extended period. Always on the move, they traveled in caravans of several decrepit covered wagons which were drawn by mangy horses. Usually they set up camp just outside a village, preferably near a source of water. Almost immediately after their arrival they fanned out into the community—the men to offer their services as "kettle menders"—actually solderers, who repaired cooking utensils—and the women with a baby, not necessarily their own, in a sling, came to beg. At their approach the women in the village called their children in from play, locked the chickens in the henhouse, and removed the laundry from the outdoor laundry lines. Gypsies had a reputation as thieves who stole everything that was not nailed down—and sometimes even that. However, I never believed the widespread rumor that gypsies stole white children and trained them to become beggars—as if they did not have enough of their own. The campsites teemed with children.

In spite of their tattered and dirty clothes gypsies managed to look extremely romantic: their dark skin, black hair, the large doleful eyes hinted at some indefinable pleasures they were keeping to themselves. Nevertheless, gypsies were an uncomfortable presence, and I could imagine that the Devil would feel quite at home with them. Of course, I had not the slightest idea what I would do if I saw him. Throw an ink pot at him, as Martin Luther had once done? A few years later, when I was in high school, my class visited the Wartburg, an old castle, where that confrontation supposedly took place. By then, however, we students were sophisticated enough to ask the guard how often he renewed the black spot on the wall.

School, as I said, did not exercise our minds or bodies. Real life began when school let out. There were no structured activities: neither Boy Scouts nor Girl Scouts, not soccer, band, or choir. Our only chore—yes, for us it was a chore—was the daily piano practice, which was exceedingly painful, both for our mother who sat next to us and had to listen to our hitting the wrong notes over and over again and for us who got slapped hard for not paying attention. Homework was negligible, and our domestic servants took care of the housework and of our little brother. The entire afternoons were free—school let out at one o'clock. We could do whatever we wanted, which was to be out and in the open. Fortunately, Koenigstein was an ideal place for us to indulge that desire. The environs were enchanting; meadows began where the tree-lined streets of the village ended, and they in turn were bordered by well-cared-for woods. Small rivulets ran through green valleys; one could almost expect to meet one of Schubert's wandering young millers to follow the meandering brooks. Over all of this towered the Feldberg, at 2,500 feet the tallest peak in the Taunus mountains. From a distance the landscape looked like one of the romantic paintings of the nineteenth-century artist Casper David Friedrich, without grandiose vistas, steep ravines or turbulent waterfalls, but with a small-scale charm of its own.

In the Middle Atlantic climate zone and at the same latitude as Newfoundland, the weather was generally cool and rainy. But as soon as the rain stopped, and we could shed the sodden, itchy loden coats that served as raincoats, I thought Summer. In June, before the first haying, the meadows were bedecked with flowers, camomiles and daisies, poppies, intensely blue cornflowers and bright buttercups, bluebells, and forget-me-nots in the marshy land. It is not nostalgia which endows this landscape of my past with so much color: the meadows look just the same today in the same climatic zone that runs from France, through Germany, into Austria. In the gardens flowers bloomed in profusion: lilies and peonies, clove-scented carnations, California poppies which close their petals at night, geraniums and narcissus, lilac and wisteria, and roses—yellow roses with the scent of tea, honey-sweet climbing roses—roses everywhere. In our yard the fruit trees bore mirabells, cherry-like yellow plums, and greengages called renny-claudes, named after a French queen (Reine Claude). Bushes bearing gooseberries, red currants, or raspberries lined the fence around the vegetable plot. In winter we usually had a couple of weeks when snow stayed on the ground. After school we pulled our sleds all the way up the Limburg highway, an hour's worth of walking, and then came down in one glorious slide. We had the whole road to ourselves; there was no oncoming traffic except an occasional horse-drawn wagon with logs for the sawmill. But even though snowfalls were sporadic, we often had spectacular hoar-frost, a fairyland of bright, glassy filaments which hung from every twig, every pine needle. We walked on tiptoe, even indoors, in order not to disturb the crystals which swayed slightly when the tree's weight shifted under the load.

By habit and inclination Germans are avid walkers. Even the most sessile burghers go for a stroll, a "Spaziergang," on a Sunday afternoon. Children walk in pairs ahead of their parents. When they meet acquaintances, men lift their hats, soldiers in uniform touch their caps, boys bow, and girls curtsy. The traditional promenade is still very much alive today, though cars, and the attraction of driving "somewhere" on a Sunday afternoon, have, of course, curtailed the number of pedestrian strollers.

As she had done in Mainz, our energetic mother took us on longer rambles through the woods. Often we ended up at one of the many forester's houses which stood in the clearings. German foresters and their wives and children all lived within their assigned territory. The men walked daily through their domain to check the growth or decay of trees and the state of the underbrush; they chopped, cleared, and reseeded. They kept count of wildlife and in general managed and protected the environment, as well as the right of people to enjoy it. Their wives, far away from any neighbors, used to serve coffee and cake to hikers, less for the sake of income, I think, than for the sake of company. The small houses were always spick-and-span. The ticking of the wall clock underscored the peacefulness but also the somnolence of the lives of those people. It was so still inside or outside, where we sat on rough-hewn benches. Today, when radios seem to blare relentlessly everywhere, it is almost impossible to recreate in one's mind the silence of those secluded places.

On our own we roamed further afield with our friends. We did not stay on the trails. We climbed up rocks and trees and explored the dangerously dilapidated secret passages under the old ruin on the hill. Sometimes we caught a glimpse of one of the deranged squatters who lived in its underground tunnels. We shrieked loudly and ran away. How fortunate that we always found an exit—it would have been so easy to lose our way. I shudder now at the thought that we could have been trapped if one of the shafts had caved in. We would never have been found. Strangely, our mother, who had watched us every minute during our stay in Mainz, no longer seemed to be concerned about our safety; our friends' parents were just as indifferent as long as the children turned up for supper. I suppose nothing in their own upbringing had made the adults aware that unsupervised children can get themselves into a lot of trouble.

Apparently our haphazard adventures got so much out of hand that we children ourselves felt the need to put the brakes on. We decided that we had to have rules and regulation and means to enforce them. Germans have a propensity to start a "Verein," that is a club, whenever two or three people want to engage in a joint activity, be it beekeeping or stargazing or whatever. Following that well-established organizing custom, we started a club that was devoted to just horsing around. First of all, we had to give it a name. Among all the synonyms for "lighthearted, friendly, cheerful," the word "fidel" seemed to be the best fit. One of the kids pointed out, however, that unfortunately the word did not imply any relationship with Kultur, and didn't we want to be considered cultured individuals? Well then, how about "Fidelio," the title of Beethoven's opera? Hurray—Club Fidelio it was—no matter that the opera's Fidelio was anything but lighthearted. Of all the by-laws which we drew up laboriously I remember only one: a member who misbehaved by whining or starting a fight was declared to be "air" for a period which depended on the severity of the transgression. The offender was admitted to club meetings, but nobody would talk to him or her. My sister was "air" most of the time, and as soon as a meeting was over she took it out on me.

MY FATHER

My father would have been appalled had he known about our explorations in the woods and around the old ruin. He did not know, and nobody bothered to tell him. He never asked us any questions beyond the traditional: how was your report card? He hardly ever listened to us or our ideas. He did not seem to be interested in what we were doing unless we proposed something he considered dangerous.

He grumbled day in and day out about the hardship of his job or about the—actually very moderate—amount of money our mother spent on the household. He taught us children bicycle riding, but he himself never got on a bike to ride along. He never went swimming, let alone ice skating or motorcycling like our uncles. He never read to us. He knew that my mother was not interested in him. She made no bones about it. "If I didn't have to drag him around with me, I would . . ." Not being wanted, he withdrew. He got up early in the morning, made himself a pot of tea, walked to the railway station, and went to his office in Frankfurt. After hours he repaired to a *Stammtisch,* where he sat with business associates till it was time to go home. He ate supper with us, sighed, and plopped down in an easy chair, where he sat silent and half-asleep till bedtime. He and my mother fought incessantly about everything and nothing; after a particularly acrimonious fight he would disappear for weeks, which made my mother nervous. Only under duress would he agree to go with us to a play or a family festivity. What he wanted was to be left alone to work on his stamp collection or to write up inventories for his business. He was somebody to be pitied, not a father one would look up to.

He was full of superstitions: when a black cat ran across his path, he spat out three times to ward off bad luck. We repeated enthusiastically after him, if only because normally spitting was strictly forbidden. He told us that if a boy or girl made a grimace when the clock strikes, his or her face would be contorted forever; we never put that gruesome prediction to the test.

Two things which scared him beyond reason were thunder and lightning and the White Slave Trade, though not concurrently. At the first sign of a thunderstorm he made us go away from windows and forbade us to touch anything made of metal, even though we had a perfectly good lightning conductor outside the house. He himself sat cowering in a corner till the storm had passed. One day a traveling circus had come to Koenigstein with a merry-go-round, a bearded lady, a couple of clowns, a high-wire act, and a few zonked-out "wild" animals. Because our mother had gone away for the day, my sister and I had to ask our father for some money for the circus. He gave us some coins and off we went. We took our time deciding what to do first; we did not want to spend all our money right away—the longer we could drag out that glorious entertainment the better. We must have been at the circus for a couple of noisy hours when our father suddenly appeared; his face was contorted with dreadful fury. He grabbed both of us by our pigtails and yanked us homeward. He was running—he who always walked so stately. He was pulling us along, shouting at us while he ran: "You idiots—didn't you see the lightning—didn't you hear the thunder? You dummies—standing out in the open!" Near our house he stopped and fumbled for the house keys. I used the moment to tear myself loose and ran ahead. In back of the house I climbed up the espalier on which Uncle Albert trained his peaches, got over the balustrade onto the veranda, and walked through an open door into the living room. From there it was only a step to the hall to slide the bolt across the entrance door. Then I sat down at the piano and began to play as loud as I could to tune out my father's shouting and door rattling. Eventually, of course, I had to let him in; I got a good spanking. I did not really mind, I deserved it—unlike the humiliation of being dragged along by my hair just because of a little thunderstorm.

I was told several years later that my father's fear of the White Slave Trade was justified. In the 1920s we simply did not believe that there was such a thing. He kept telling us that it was an international conspiracy which lured young girls into Houses of Joy. "You don't know what's going on in the world," he said when we ridiculed his allegations, "I hear true stories; I know." "You would know," scoffed my mother, "you are the one who frequents Houses of Joy; admit it." What was wrong with Houses of Joy? Why didn't he want us to be joyful too? We did not know that it was a figure of speech for a brothel, but we did not know what a brothel was either. He kept on, telling us a "true story": how a young girl attending a theater performance with a companion was spirited away when the latter went to the restroom during the intermission. People in the next row later recalled that a man had come up and invited the girl to join him for refreshments in the lobby. When her friend returned from the restroom, the girl had vanished, and nobody ever saw her again. "She's probably in a brothel in Constantinople," concluded my father, "and that's where you will end up if you don't watch out!" When I was in college he was fuming when I told him about vacation jobs I was going to apply for. "You are not going to Finland as a tutor—that's where the White Slave Trade has its headquarters. You are not going to take a temporary job as a secretary in Switzerland—with all those borders it is so easy to whisk an innocent girl into Italy or France or Austria. You are not going to Iceland to help with the haying." Probably he envisioned a White Slave Trader lurking among the geysers. My mother could have supported me in my plans by simply disregarding his objections to anything that was not totally conventional. But she was afraid that she would be held responsible, by my father and everybody else, if I came to grief.

$\mathcal{D}$uring our childhood in Koenigstein, my mother did not object to our outdoor adventures, but she kept controlling what we ate. No synthetic food such as margarine, no canned food, not even the canned pineapple the relatives in America sent us. She selected the patterns for our garments, which the local seamstress was to cobble together. We were not allowed any say. On the other hand, we had carte blanche to read virtually everything we came across. Such freedom, unimaginable for today's worried parents, was not indicative of our parents' ultra-liberalism. There were built-in barriers which protected us young readers. The bookcases of middle-class families did not contain anything but "classics" which, by definition, were educational and uplifting. They were treasured status symbols—regardless of their literary merits. These were the books which we were permitted, even encouraged, to read from cover to cover. In fact, they were the only printed matter to which we had access. Libraries were few and far between. Most likely the librarian knew the young readers who came into the library, and if one of them had been observed rummaging in the "adult" section, the librarian would have stopped him or her and reported him to his parents. There were no newsstands or checkout counters displaying lurid magazine covers. Porn and girlie magazines were kept under the counter, and there was little danger that we would ever be exposed to that kind of smut.

I still have my reading list of those years: Schiller and Goethe, Gottfried Keller, Conrad Ferdinand Meyer, Moerike, Selma Lagerloef, Charles Dickens, and Walter Scott—and countless other authors who are all but forgotten today. Ernest Hemingway's *Farewell to Arms* was serialized in the local twice-a-week newspaper. I waited at the corner for the newsboy, so that I could read every new sequence before somebody else got his or her hands on the paper.

The only category of reading matter which was strictly forbidden consisted of backstairs romances, Nancy Drew–type teenage girls' books, and Karl May's works. They were not "Kultur." In fact, Karl May was forbidden reading for most children. I cannot imagine why. The books definitely were not pornographic, far from it. They dealt with the adventures of the noble Indians in North America. Perhaps it was the author's disreputable life that set one's parents against him. In the 1880s he was a small-town bookkeeper who landed in jail because he had committed fraud and robbed the poor-boxes in the churches. With a lot of time on his hands he began inventing tales of the Indians which were so convincing and so vivid that he soon attracted an enormous readership. Everybody thought that he had spent years in North America and observed the Indians at first hand. Still, his writings were kept away from youngsters, and it is only now, over a hundred years later, that people are no longer embarrassed to admit that they enjoy Karl May. These days, when the German tour buses stop at the Grand Canyon, it is a safe bet that most of the travelers come with a Karl May book to orient themselves in Indian country.

Aunt Lisbeth did indeed invite me a second time to stay with her family in St. Moritz during the winter. It was even better than during the preceding year. I was a year older, I was physically well, and I was far more secure in their midst. Aunt Lisbeth took me and her nine-year-old daughter skiing—mostly Nordic skiing, that is. Nobody did any downhill except a few young Norwegian daredevils. Even in St. Moritz, the most exclusive and fashionable winter resort in the world, there were no lifts or even rope tows, no trails, no pistes, no runs. We climbed the slopes with skins tied to the underside of our skis and, after removing the skins, skied down in deep powder. Christies were all but unknown. We executed telemarks to brake our runs. In retrospect, that second winter was the best of the three I was to spend with my lovable relatives. A year later there was a foreboding of an impending tragedy. Family gossip had it that the marriage of my uncle and aunt was in danger of breaking up. Aunt Lisbeth had become very attached to a sculptor, a married man to boot. She had taken up sculpturing herself and spent a good deal of her time in her room shaping heads and bodies from lumps of wet clay. My uncle, practically monosyllabic, was in no mood to organize the lighthearted sleigh rides or other cheerful entertainment of earlier years. I had never come across emotional upheaval, least of all a romantic entanglement involving adults, and I found it extremely upsetting that my aunt as much as admitted to me how deeply she was smitten. One day when she took me along on a drive to a crafts workshop, way out of town, she asked the perfunctory questions: how do you like your teachers? and so on. Chatting, I told her of the crush—typical for a twelve-year-old girl—which I had on one of the teachers—I do not even remember whether it was a male or female. Aunt Lisbeth replied, apparently forgetting to whom she was talking: "Don't ever fall for a married man—he'll always go back to his wife." Obviously she did not realize that it was a confession of sorts to a child.

In March, my Mainz grandfather joined us for a brief holiday. When it was time for him to go home it was decided that I was to go back with him. I was desolate. I did not want to go home before Aunt Lisbeth left, especially since I had a feeling that this was the last winter I was going to be with her and her family. Of course, I could not tell her that; after all the wonderful things she had done for me it would have been disgustingly ungrateful to beg for more time. I put on a smiling face when I said goodbye at the railway station, but as soon as the train started moving, I crouched down in a corner and started to cry. My grandfather pretended not to notice, or perhaps he was already ogling an upholstered, overdressed, over-rouged and, in my opinion, very common woman across the aisle. Ten minutes later, when the train stopped in Pontresina, he had already moved next to her and did not notice that I stepped out of the train. I was going to telephone my aunt and beg her to come and get me. I just could not bear to be separated from her and her family. But I had no money for a telephone call. I stood on the platform, irresolute and forlorn. The train conductor came along: "What are you standing here for? The train is leaving in a minute. Get in!" He shoved me up the stairs into the railway car. Sometime later my grandfather introduced me to his new acquaintance, who, he said, was an opera singer. In Zurich, where we were to spend the night, he ordered room service supper for me; he and the lady were going out for dinner, he said.

Two years later Aunt Lisbeth died of leukemia.

After the eighth grade of the Taunus Realschule, most of my classmates immediately entered the working world. At age fourteen or so childhood was over and adulthood began. There was no interim, no teenage adolescence. The transition was immediate and sharp and without any rites of passage except confirmation in the Lutheran church. The Roman Catholic children went to their first Holy Communion when they were six years old; the little girls looked angelic in their frilly white outfits, and their families celebrated the occasion with a big joyous party. By contrast, the Lutheran confirmation was a somber affair for the young people on the threshold of adulthood. The boys wore dark suits, and the girls were in black dresses, newly made or bought for the occasion. Well worth spending money on, it was said, because they would get a lot of use out of them at all the funerals they would have to attend—an alarming augury for the future. Except for the religious ceremony, there were only a few markers signifying the end of childhood. Girls put their hair up, and boys started to wear long pants. Instead of using the familiar "Du," our teachers and everybody else now addressed us with the formal "Sie." Yesterday the maid would say, "Deine Mutter sagt, Du solltest . . ."; the next day she changed to "Ihre Mutter sagt, Sie sollten . . ." On leaving school, some girls went into service, and the boys were apprenticed to craftsmen or tradesmen. Some of my friends who were going to continue their education were sent off to boarding schools; others, like myself, were enrolled as day students in the local convent school. My mother apparently was determined to keep me under her wings as long as possible, even at the cost of mediocre schooling.

*T*he Sisters meant well, and they were in general far more interested in us girls than the teachers in the old school had been. I
admired their singleness of heart, their unquestioning devotion,
and their effort to teach us what they thought we ought to know.
The ninth grade was the uppermost grade in that school, and the
parents of the boarding students expected that year to give their
daughters the polish which would serve them well in their future
lives as wives of prosperous, solid husbands. An inordinate
amount of time was spent on perfecting this image: sewing, and
embroidering doilies, to be put on top of yet more doilies for the
overstuffed furniture of the girls' prospective future homes. After
Christmas vacations, one of the students brought back a kind of
hanging to be worked in needlepoint. It had a design of little
cherubs floating around with garlands in their chubby hands. The
piece vanished after class; when it re-appeared, the Sewing Class
Sister had re-designed the original, so that the little cherubs were
now in robes. "You would not want to have unclad figures in your
house," she told the startled girl. Physical education and health
were taken seriously; one Sister took us, crocodile style, on long

walks. When the girls complained, she told them that one day they would remember her with gratitude, because she helped them to develop a healthy body "so that you don't become sickly women and a burden to your husbands." Two Sisters even took us to the swimming pool and made us get into the ice-cold water that came straight from a spring. The pool was situated at the bottom of a high rocky hill. The local louts used to climb to the top and ogle the girls during the ladies' hours. To forestall such impropriety, one Sister ascended the rock and sat herself down on top with a large club in her hand to keep voyeurs away, while the other Sister watched over us from the side of the pool. Not that any Peeping Toms could have seen much: our bathing suits had elbow-length sleeves and knickers that went down to the knees.

The boarding students told us that they were not even allowed to look at their own legs when they were taking their Saturday night bath: the bath tub was covered with a large white cloth which had a small opening at one end. The bather was to slip through that opening into the water and wash her limbs underneath the cover. At the convent it was strictly forbidden to look at one's body from the chin down.

Once a week a dance teacher was imported from Frankfurt to teach us the latest steps. Before the class started the nuns scattered slivers of floor wax over the polished hardwood floor, so that when we danced in our stocking feet we were polishing their floors at the same time. One Sister sat at the piano and played the latest hits from the sheet music the dance teacher brought along: "Yes, we have no bananas," and "What do you do with your knee, my dear Hans, when we dance, when we dance, when we dance ..." Of course, there were no boys—we took turns in partnering, whether it was a waltz, a tango, or the Charleston.

I demonstrated at home for the family and the maids, who were impressed by my worldliness. "Now that you have learned all the dance steps," declared my mother, "I'll take you to a real dance hall where you can dance with real young men, not with those convent girls." I do not think that my parents had ever been to a dance. As a young girl, my mother may have been at some dancing parties in private homes. The War and the post-War years were far too grim

for my parents even to contemplate going to something as frivolous as a social dance—quite apart from the fact that neither of
them had any bent for lighthearted entertainments. My mother
probably had no idea what a public dancing place looked like. All
she knew was that a bankrupt hotel on the road toward Frankfurt
had lately started Sunday afternoon "tea dances" in an attempt to
make some money. The location of the place was such that it could
be reached only on foot or by car. Cars were still a rarity; with the
exception of automobile salesmen and the occasional high roller,
few young people had one, or even the use of one. Those youths
who did were considered affluent—potential big spenders who
might be attracted to those "tea dances." Actually, the hotel was
more like a common roadhouse, with the right amount of glitz to
impress its prospective clientele.

One Sunday afternoon my mother made us all dress up and
walk a mile or so up the hill to that hotel. As usual, my sister and I
walked in front of my mother and my grumbling father. A dance
floor in the center of the hotel lounge was surrounded by small tables and chairs where we sat down. The air was smoky, the décor
garish, and the band sadly uninspired. My parents ordered coffee
and cake, which we ate as slowly as possible. Meanwhile my
mother kept an eye out for somebody, anybody, who would ask me
to dance. Nobody came. The unattached young men knew better
than to waste their time on children who were watched over by
mom and pop. They homed right in on the come-hither girls in
their bright plumage who had come to the dance in unchaperoned
groups. "People probably think that you don't know how to dance,"
said my mother. "Go and show them—the two of you get up and go
out on the dance floor." It was a humiliating performance: a fifteen-
year-old and a thirteen-year-old shuffling around among a crowd of
twenty-something youths on the make. Neither we nor anybody
else could make out what we were doing there. When the dance
was over we returned to my parents' table and continued to wait
without hope for relief from this gloomy afternoon. Finally my father got up and said he'd had enough: "Let's try one more time,"
persisted my mother, and dispatched us again to dance. After that
she gave up too, and then all of us walked home in the dark. The

dreary experiment was repeated a few more times—no matter that my father and we girls protested—before it was given up for good.

Besides "accomplishment" classes, the curriculum at the convent included literature, history, math, and science. One of the Sisters even demonstrated a Geissler tube, an early forerunner of the now ubiquitous gas discharge tubes, which was more advanced than anything we had been exposed to in the previous school. Literature, however, was somewhat skimpy. All books that were on the Index—the books Catholics were forbidden to read—were out. It seemed that many of the books I had read, and particularly everything written by Goethe—our great Goethe—were proscribed. One day I saw Goethe's Collected Works in the library of our physician, a good friend and a devout Catholic. I asked him how he reconciled the Church's interdict with his literary taste. He said that as an educated man he was exempt from the Index. What puzzled me then, and still puzzles me, is this: how can you become an educated person without reading these books?

I tried a new tack with the Sisters. "My mother says," I protested. "We will not discuss what your mother says," replied Mater Cornelia, "Goethe is on the Index because he led an amoral life. He only married his mistress at the eve of the battle of Jena. That has been documented. But take Schiller . . ." Goethe and Schiller, who were contemporaries, were the two brightest stars in the German classical literary firmament. They were worshipped like deities. Every event, no matter how trite, was an occasion to quote them— and thereby trivialize both their fine poetry and their wisdom. Suppose you told your neighbor, please, to keep his dog off your lawn. With pompous one-upmanship he or she would put you down: "Even a sage would be inclined / to love a dog well trained to mind—Goethe, Faust, Part I." Schiller wrote numerous historical dramas; unfortunately he was also an obsessive rhymester who produced a myriad of theatrical ballads with preposterous verses. And because the rhymes made memorizing easy, schoolchildren were forced to learn dozens of those ballads by heart. "The Song of the Bell," I still remember, began with: "From the heated brow— sweat must freely flow, so the work the master showeth, yet the blessing Heaven bestoweth . . ." This goes on for twelve pages describing not only the process of making a bell, but reciting the entire history of the bell maker and his family. The Sisters were partial to Schiller, who led an exemplary life and glorified housewifely virtues. "The gloss and the shine to the gold she adds ever—and resteth never"—a verse that was quoted to us over and over again. What was not mentioned was that all that polishing—plus a dozen or so childbirths—killed that workaholic in her prime.

Schiller's dramas were also devoid of romance. Thus, when the local movie house showed a filmed version of *Wallenstein,* one of his historical plays, it was considered an educational presentation worth attending. Our class was marched off to a matinee performance accompanied by Mater Cornelia, who took a seat next to the light switch. The moment a youthful warrior approached a young maiden and the caption read (that was in the age of silent films!) something like: "Oh, you angel, let me gaze at you once more before I ride out into battle . . . ," on went the light for a minute or two, until passion subsided or the hero was killed, whatever came first.

At last the year in the convent school came to an end, and a decision had to be made where my further education was to take place. After the dispirited time served in my prior schools, I would have liked to go to a progressive institution such as Dr. Kurt Hahn's Bodenseeschule, one of many that had been started after the War. But I was not asked what I wanted. I was to go to the Schiller School, a girls' school in Frankfurt. I was to board with the Floberts and come home on weekends.

I did not know—neither did my mother—that this decision heralded a definite change in our relationship; the future would not be a continuation of the past, in which she had made every single decision for me. I anticipated that the new school would be just another educational institution, though on a higher intellectual level than the ones I had attended until then. My mother believed that she would not only continue being the dominant influence in my life: she would now launch me on my way to achieving fame and fortune, for myself as well as for her, whose ambition had been thwarted early on. "Take Mme. Curie as a role model," she would tell me, "she has mastered mathematics and physics, the most abstract sciences. If you apply yourself you can become another Mme. Curie and invent radium!" She must have known that one cannot become a genius just by applying oneself; but I am sure that she did not worry about such a complication and instead conjured up a vision of herself and me acclaimed as the outstanding women of the century.

Both of us were wrong: the new school was not only far more stimulating than I had imagined it to be; it encouraged, even demanded, emancipation of the students from the standards of bourgeois conventionality. Inevitably, I began to break away from my mother's dominance and to question the values she and her circle espoused.

The suitcase that I was to take to the Floberts in Frankfurt held, among the usual supplies, half a dozen raw eggs, which my mother had carefully wrapped up in my school clothes. Every morning, she instructed me, I was to take an egg and make one hole in the top and one in the bottom and suck out the viscous fluid. A new supply of raw eggs accompanied me to Frankfurt after every weekend I spent at home. That way my mother felt assured that I would get the nourishment which the parsimonious Floberts were unlikely to provide. Of course, they must not know about it— I would have to dispose of the eggshells on the way to school. The Floberts had no children; according to family gossip, they had waited for months to consummate their marriage. It was said—I have no idea who spread that legend—that Queen Victoria had started this delaying ploy, which was continued by her descendants, to prove that humankind was not subject to animal desires. Still, she managed to produce a large family, while Aunt Flora and Uncle Albert, who aspired to the decorum of the Victorian era, or at least their image of the period, remained childless. My mother thought that they did not know how much food a growing girl needs. I think they knew perfectly well, but they really had very little money, and most of it went to sustain a so-called high-bourgeois standard of living. They skimped on food and other "non-essentials" while maintaining the outward appearance of middle-class comfort. It was a life of genteel poverty, of make-believe which not only they but most of their contemporaries lived after the inflation had robbed them of their savings. Like "everybody else," the Floberts subscribed to a chamber music series but, to save the streetcar fare, walked home after the concerts, two elderly people strolling through the dark streets. Aunt Flora had her coats turned inside out when the material on the outside had frayed, and her hats were periodically re-shaped so she could pretend she had a "new" wardrobe. They could afford only one maid-servant, Gretchen, a slightly retarded woman whom they had plucked out from a mental institution. Whenever visitors were expected, Gretchen had to dress up in a silly little white apron and a frilly cap to make her appear, not as the maid-of-all-work which she was, but as a parlor maid and part of a large staff.

For most callers though, Aunt Flora was "not at home," a useful phrase which suited both the visitors who were fulfilling a social obligation and the lady of the house who might not particularly want to receive anybody. She had a spyglass mounted outside the drawing room window, which allowed her to watch, without being observed, who was entering her house and also who went in and out at the neighbors. Still, making calls was a social obligation which people were expected to discharge. The older generation especially thought it rude to use the telephone to enquire about somebody's health or well-being. One had to call in person and deposit one's visiting card on a small silver tray proffered by the maid. A young man who walked a young lady home from a party, and who had not been introduced to her parents, must "leave his card" at their home the following Sunday. No matter what their other plans for Sunday were, or how far out of town they lived, the poor guys had to appear in person and leave their cards if the daughter of the house would ever again be allowed to go out with them.

Aunt Flora suffered from high blood pressure and spent most of her days lying on a couch in the living room. "Comme les grandes horizontales," she said half mockingly, though there was absolutely nothing in her tall, gaunt figure, or in her blood-veined face, to invite comparison with the great courtesans of the French fin de siè-cle society. She claimed to be a descendant of one of Napoleon's brothers and his morganatic wife; as "proof" she showed off a miniature portrait of a lovely lady, her alleged ancestress, whoever she might have been.

I did not take all these pretensions very seriously. The Floberts were old people—let them have their illusions of a glorious past. At age fifteen I felt very much a member of the younger generation.

1. Clara Lahnstein,
the author's mother,
1909 or 1910.

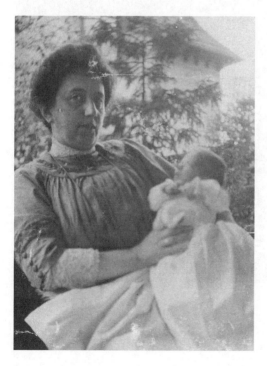

2. The author
and her grand-
mother Lahnstein,
1911.

3. The author's father, Fritz Schmitz, with Doris, 1911.

4. The author (left) and her sister, 1913.

5. Great-Uncle Albert with young members of the family, 1915.

6. The author (left) and her sister, poolside, 1917.

7. Sitting on a wine vat at the home of vintner relatives, 1916–17.

8. An excursion during the year in the convent (ca. 1925). The author is in the front row, second from the right, turned away from the camera.

9. The author at the time of her marriage, 1937.

10. Doris and Peter Drucker, 1942.

11. The author in 1995.

*H*aving passed the entrance examination for the tenth grade, I was told to report to the school principal for orientation early in the morning of the first day of class. A tall man, his hands stretched out in greeting, strode toward me and boomed: "May God punish England!" I was taken aback; my first reaction was to ask: "Why?" My rehearsed greeting, "Good morning, Herr Direktor," did not seem to fit the occasion either. Fortunately, he enlightened me. "You are to reply 'May God punish England'—we all need to implore the good Lord to hear us." Thereupon he sat down and had me fill out forms. Herr Direktor B., I heard later, was a displaced person; his hometown in one of the Eastern provinces had been ceded to Poland under the Treaty of Versailles or, as we were told to call it, the Ignominy of Versailles. He had come West to Frankfurt rather than stay on as a member of a suppressed minority under the despised "Pollacks," whom he considered to be a lower species of mankind. Ever after he yearned for the restitution of pre-War Germany and for revenge against England, which he singled out as the instigator of all his troubles.

After that strange introduction, I was sent to my classroom and assigned a desk. In a few moments a teacher entered, and, as was the custom in Germany, all of us students rose to our feet. (We also stood up when a teacher left the classroom after a lesson.) But instead of sitting down again, the girls, still on their feet, began to sing a folksong of many verses. I found out that in the new school the day always started with a song: on the spur of the moment we might pick a heart-wrenching lament about the pains of unrequited love, a ballad about an abandoned girl, the sorrow of parting from one's sweetheart, or a merry marching song—we had a large repertoire. These were the songs favored by the Wandervoegel—a romantic back-to-nature youth movement which rejected all features of urban civilization. With its strong nationalist component it was warmly supported within the school.

However, neither the teachers nor the students shared the chauvinism which the principal exhibited; unlike him, they did not want the return of the Kaiser and of his industrialist and merchants-of-death friends. They proposed a romantic nationalism founded on the innate essence of the Germanic people. It included all the elements of a glorious past: the Neolithic Nibelungs; the courtly minstrels; the sturdy craftsmen of the medieval cities and the wayfaring journeymen; the sober philosophers of the eighteenth century; Goethe and Schiller; the patriotic Queen Luise of the Napoleonic wars, as well as a solid peasantry anchored in the soil. All were part of the Germanic heritage and had to be amalgamated to create the future state, which was to be populated by blond and strong Nordic-type men and women who remained young forever.

I was astounded by the fierceness with which the girls and their parents defended their political beliefs. My family was basically apolitical; they claimed to have a lukewarm interest in the Weimar Republic and voted for the Democratic Party, slightly left of center. Nevertheless, my mother leaned toward the Conservatives and kept quoting the old Chancellor von Bismarck, who had said that the only way to deal with Democrats is to shoot them. She saw nothing contrarian in her way of thinking. I would guess that the parents of most of my classmates voted for the right of center German National Party. The Left talked of a permanent accommodation with France in the spirit of Romain Rolland—a widely read and very influential French author of the twenties. The Right rejected internationalism and pacifism and argued for a Germany that would go it alone.

Yet in spite of their political fervor my classmates distanced themselves from the National Socialist rabble-rousers on the Right as much as my parents distanced themselves from the Communist rabble-rousers on the Left. No doubt some of the girls would later become enthusiastic Hitler followers, but during our school years there was nothing but contempt for the pimply Nazi louts. One classmate told us that a young man who came to pick her up for a party arrived at her house in full Nazi uniform, including an armband with a large swastika. He raised his arm in greeting and shouted "Heil Hitler!" "Ach, Walter," she had said, "put that silly arm down." The boy's face turned purple but he said nothing. Three years later he denounced her as an "enemy of the people." She had to flee at once, leaving her home in the dark of night.

In Germany there certainly was latent anti-Semitism, but in the Schiller School it was hardly an issue. So many of the students came from mixed marriages that the children themselves decided where they wanted to belong. Such mixing included interdenominational marriages between Catholics and Protestants as well as marriages between Jews and Christians. Actually, it was so common for Jews to marry Christians that the rabbinate feared the virtual disappearance of German Jewry within three or, at most, four generations. It was only when Hitler came to power that anybody with a Jewish parent or grandparent was designated a Jew who must be exterminated for the greater glory of the German race.

It so happened that one of the students, a product of a marriage between a Jew and a Christian, personified the ideal of German womanhood. A striking tall, blond girl, Helene Mayer was a world-class sports figure. As a junior in high school, she won the Olympic Gold Medal for fencing. When she returned from the Games she was a celebrity. She displayed a letter: "Dear Mr. School Principal," it said, "Please excuse Helene Mayer's absence from school the day before yesterday. At my request she stayed on in Berlin a day longer so that she could attend the banquet I gave for the German participants at the Olympic Games." The letter was signed by the Reich president von Hindenburg, the erstwhile field marshal of the German armies.

All of us would have given an arm and a leg to be like Helene—when, in fact, most of us girls were rather plain-looking types. We disdained the camouflage of cosmetics—we who were set on creating a new, purer Germany. Flattering clothes were for airheads; we, the advocates of artlessness, were not going to be influenced by current fashions. We wore shapeless peasant-style dresses made from an intensely blue fabric which was imprinted with a white overall design. All of us, that is, except for me. My mother was adamant—she was not going to allow me to wear those garments. She claimed that they were "not ladylike"—of course, they were not. That was the whole point. Other mothers may have shared her opinion; but wiser than she, they let their daughters have their minor rebellion, while my mother obstinately made me wear—in tenth grade!—the childish smocked dresses stitched together by the Koenigstein seamstress.

I had been rather indifferent to clothes until then; they did not mean all that much to me. But at that time I really craved those blue and white dresses. I thought of them day and night. If I had one, I thought, I would not quite stand out so much as a newcomer in the Schiller School. Peer pressure can be very powerful when one is fifteen years old. I cried, I protested, I made all kinds of dramatic pronouncements—to no avail.

I never forgot the episode; it left a deeper split between my mother and myself than I would admit at the time.

Sixty years later, passing by a shop window, I saw a dress that was a reasonable facsimile of the long-ago school outfit; without a moment's hesitation I bought it, never even considering that the style might not be suitable for me at that stage of my life.

In tenth grade I was barely aware that my mother's arbitrariness, not only in this but in other matters as well, was getting uncontrollable. Years later she was diagnosed as a manic depressive whose eccentricity could be explained by her mood swings. But at age fifteen, I had never heard of mental illness, and, even if I had, I would not have admitted to myself that she was afflicted. To escape was not only the natural reaction of a teenager—it became a necessity for me if I wanted to grow up normal. Fortunately the Schiller School offered physical as well as intellectual escape routes.

𝒯he educational program for all grades called for frequent and prolonged excursions to different parts of Germany which were to be studied in depth. We visited museums and monuments to learn about the local history and the tradition of the inhabitants; we observed the plant and animal life. We were taught the geology of the region and other special features. One excursion led us to Stuttgart and its surroundings—the beautiful old convent of Maulbronn, the medieval walled city of Dinkelsbuehl, and Ulm with its grand cathedral. Another time we went to Munich—at the time of the Oktoberfest—to visit the great art galleries, the lovely baroque churches, the Deutsche Museum (the model for the Museum of Science and Industry in Chicago, where visitors can actuate programmed science experiments), and Nymphenburg and Schwanstein, the preposterous castles of mad King Ludwig. Having dutifully absorbed so much Kultur, we concluded our trip by repairing with the teacher to the Rathskeller and an evening of beer and jollity. There was no prohibition against drinking by juveniles. From age fourteen on young people drank beer or wine in public as casually as today's youngsters drink Coke. Another trip took us to

Bamberg, Wuerzburg, and the lovely small towns along the upper reaches of the Main River. We strolled through small baroque palaces which once belonged to the many sovereigns of secular and clerical principalities in the area. Most of the buildings and the park-like gardens were in a state of melancholic decay, which the frolicking sculptured cherubs among the overgrown boxwood did not seem to notice.

The excursions were not meant to be recreational; besides their educational aspect they served another, not so obvious, agenda: to mold the thirty or so girls in each grade into one cohesive unit which performed more or less at the same level. Almost all of us came from middle-class families, but there was still a clear division between the children of professionals or academics and those whose fathers were in business. To bridge the gap, teachers from time to time moved an entire class for a week to a country cabin which belonged to the school. Communal living and concentrated study away from the distractions of family and friends, it was believed, would lower the perception of differences and make for greater harmony and unity of purpose in the classroom.

A more ambitious citywide program, run by the city of Frankfurt, was likewise intended to bring children of different backgrounds close to one another. It was a naïve proposition which was doomed to fail: proximity did not promote equality of any kind. The place where this was going to happen was a huge camp in the woods north of the city; attendance was mandatory. We privileged girls should have been moved by the physical and spiritual poverty of some of the children with whom we shared living space. However, we could not relate to them. We spent a miserable week squashing bedbugs in our bunks and chasing rats out of the barracks where we slept.

Our regular field trips—and there were at least two a year—led us to parts of Germany which we might not have seen otherwise. Before the automobile became a household appliance, Germans did not travel as easily as they do today. Once in a lifetime, perhaps on a honeymoon, they might follow Goethe's footsteps and go to Italy to visit all the Travel Guide's three-star monuments. The kind of casual traveling to which we have become accustomed simply did not exist. Train travel was tedious. On arrival at their destination the passengers were tired and covered with soot which was discharged by the coal-fired locomotives. There were no motels; lodgings were either very expensive or very primitive.

The British and the Americans did not seem to mind the inconveniences and engaged in foreign travel. In England there was the tradition of the young milord who was sent on a grand tour of the Continent, or even of the world. Americans came to Europe to visit what they imagined to be the picturesque homestead of their ancestors. At one time descendants of my grandfather's siblings— my mother's cousins—came from New York to visit us in Koenigstein. They landed at our doorstep like a bunch of exotic and colorful birds. We showed them the ruined fortress; they claimed to be fascinated by our vegetable garden—"Is that how peas grow? I've got to take a picture." And they wanted to know whether we—at the latitude of Duluth!—also grew bananas. After they left we made fun of their gaudy outfits—German women over thirty never, ever, wore anything but decently muted colors.

When we went sightseeing it was only on day trips: my mother took us to Worms and Speyer to visit the great cathedrals and the famous religious sites of the once-thriving Jewish communities, to Wetzlar, where Goethe dallied with the virtuous Lotte, and to other nearby sites of historical relevance. My grandfather's idea of a treat was to take us on a boat ride down the Rhine to Coblenz, from where we returned by train. To do it once was enjoyable, but to do it every year became boring. We did not dare say so. During the first two hours of the ride the boat stopped at every one of the wine-producing villages—Eltville and Ruedesheim and many more—so that the passengers could sample the local vintage. Beyond Bingen, where the Rhine enters a narrow gorge, the current flowed faster, and the boat began bobbing up and down. By then the passengers were thoroughly stewed. Sitting around a large table on deck, they linked arms and all of them together kept swaying sideways, back and forth, to counteract the rocking of the boat. They seemed to find this exceedingly hilarious. After a while a tall rock came into view; that was the Lorelei promontory; according to a legend it used to be the seat of a beautiful maiden who lured many a boatman to his death in the river. At the sight of the rock our stupidly grinning co-passengers burst, as if hypnotized, into the famous Lorelei song:

> I cannot tell why this imagined
> Despair has fallen on me;
> The ghost of an ancient legend
> That will not let me be.

—the first stanza of a long, melancholic ballad that ends with the drowning of the lovesick, bewitched boatman. After they had croaked out all the verses, they fell into a tearful Weltschmerz which lasted till the boat ride was over.

Except for those short trips, we traveled only to visit relatives. After Aunt Lisbeth's death, Uncle Sigi had moved back to Argentina. Every other year he and the children came to Europe for a stay of several weeks. He took a suite of rooms in a luxury hotel and invited scores of his and his late wife's relatives to stay. Once, during our Christmas vacations, my sister and I were his guests at the French Riviera. I had never been south of the Alps; like most people from the cold grey North I was intoxicated by the sun, the soft air, and the enticing scents. Yellow lemons hung among dark leaves, palm trees stretched into the sky, and flowers were in bloom in the middle of winter. Flower shops in Frankfurt sometimes featured a slim spray of mimosas; at the Riviera, clusters upon clusters grew on tall bushes. I could not tear myself away. I was reading at the time Rilke's "Malte Laurids Brigge"; the lyric sentiments of the story and the sensitivity of the little yellow mimosas seemed to be of one piece. At the slightest touch the soft round puffs withdrew into rough greenish balls—a symbolical parallel to the seclusion of the touchy protagonist of the story.

My uncle had brought his Hispano-Suiza automobile and a driver over from Argentina: in that beautiful luxury car he took us on breathtaking drives along the coast or on the Grande Corniche, the high road which curves along the steep coastal mountains. The Riviera was then an enclave of the super rich; there were no tourists. Visitors stayed for weeks, perhaps months, in their villas or in the grand-hotels of Nice or Cannes, which were the most elegant places imaginable. The ladies in our party ogled a famous actress who sported a black suit made of the skin of unborn lambs. How disgustingly decadent—and how beautiful!

Two years later, when Uncle Sigi and his entourage were due for another visit in Europe, my mother decided that for once his—and her late sister's—children should have a different experience; instead of living in the lap of luxury they ought to see how the other half—no, make that the other 98 percent—of the world lives. She would rent a simple summer place on the Baltic Coast, which would be my uncle's headquarters. Early in the spring she went on an inspection tour; a seaside resort is never at its best in cold and blustery weather, and the Baltic Coast, which is bleak even in the middle of summer, was utterly depressing. But my mother found what seemed to her an adequate house and informed Uncle Sigi of her plan. She did not hear from him and assumed that he was in agreement. When the boat from Argentina docked in Hamburg, she was at the quay to escort him and the children to the vacation rental at the Baltic Sea.

"How far is the house from the golf course?" Uncle Sigi wanted to know. My mother was dumbfounded; she had a vague idea that golf was a game like croquet in which the players hit a little ball with a stick. She remembered that there was a lush meadow right behind the house; a good place for croquet or golf, if you got somebody to cut the tall grass. "How many holes?" continued Uncle Sigi. "No holes, absolutely no holes!" said my mother indignantly. "It is a very well-kept place, I assure you. I would never have taken it if I had seen any holes in the ground—much too dangerous for the children."

Uncle Sigi, I am sure, never had any intentions of becoming a victim of my mother's reform scheme; he told her to cancel the lease—he would reimburse her for any expenses. He and his children were going to stay at a Grand Hotel in the Thuringian Forest, where he had already booked rooms, and we were invited to join him there as his guests. My sister and I protested; we had looked forward to a sea-and-sand summer. But my mother said we had to go to inland Thuringia, and that was that. If we put up a good face and stopped complaining, she promised she would allow us to spend the next vacations at a place of our own choice.

I did not have to deliberate long: during the Christmas vacations I was going to go skiing with a group of girls from my school.

The Schiller School owned a small cabin in a godforsaken valley, far away in the foothills of the southern Alps. Getting there was not easy: we traveled all night by a cheap (and slow) train and then skied for eight hours across two high ridges before descending toward our goal. There was no road; we followed markers stuck in the snow. Everybody in our group, including a young male teacher and two college women who were to be our chaperones, carried a backpack which held everything we would need for the two weeks' vacation: there was no store in our valley. Our destination, a typical alpine one-room peasant cottage, was at the far end of a tiny village. It had none of the amenities we were used to. A kerosene lamp provided the sole illumination. There was an outhouse in back; water came from a spring high up in the mountains and flowed into a trough outside the front door. It froze over every night; in the morning we climbed down from the hayloft in which we slept and hacked away chunks of ice and melted them on the stove. It was so cold that winter that the milk we fetched for breakfast from the nearest farmhouse froze in the pails while we carried them to our cabin. But the snow was deep and powdery, and the skiing was marvelous. We were on the slopes from morning till sunset. We skied on wooden skis—there were no others—which were very long and heavy. They were also quite inflexible and apt to break into two pieces when they hit a rock or a tree stump that was hidden in the snow. We always carried spare metal tips as temporary attachments to broken skis; without a curved tip it would have been very difficult to navigate in deep snow.

A broken ski was an inconvenience; a broken leg in that isolated valley would have been a great deal worse. In our naïve illusion of sharing, if only temporarily, the simple way of life of the local peasants, we never thought of the dangers to which we were exposed. Teenagers overlook the possibility of calamities. But our elders should have known better. One of us might have come down with appendicitis or another illness requiring instant medical attention. There was no radio, no telegraph to summon help. It would take a messenger a whole day on skis to reach the nearest city. And would a doctor undertake the long trip to our valley? Even if he started out, would he arrive in time to save a life? And what about the acute fire danger in the flimsy hay-filled cottage? A spark from the wood-burning stove or from an overturned kerosene lamp would set the place on fire in an instant. If it happened at night, would we be able to escape with our lives? Nobody worried; neither the Schiller School administration which organized the trips, nor our young teacher, nor the two coeds. Not even our parents were worried. Their total lack of concern was inexplicable. At home they guarded their daughters obsessively against the greatest danger they could imagine: seduction and premarital sex. Was that the only danger they envisaged? If they traveled at all, our mothers, who were adolescents in the late 1890s, only went to the homes of friends or relatives, where they were as protected as at home. In the 1920s they probably assumed that our teacher and the chaperones would substitute for the watchful uncles and aunts and keep seducers away. I do not think it entered our parents' minds that their daughters could be exposed to physical risks. Sons, yes, but girls, never!

One day, fifty years later, I received a telephone call from a grandson who wanted to invite me to a school play in which he had a small acting role. I excused myself—I would be away at the time trekking in the Himalayas. "Really?" he asked incredulously. "Didn't your mother tell you about my plans?" "No, she never did." After we had finished our conversation I turned to my husband. "If your grandmother had planned to go hiking in the Himalayas, don't you think that topic would have been discussed back and forth for weeks within the family?" "Of course—but you know, that problem never came up." Just as the problem of our risky expeditions never came up in the 1920s.

Perhaps it was just as well that my parents were as nonchalant as all the other parents. Otherwise they might not have allowed me to go, two years later, on an even more challenging ski trip to Switzerland. There, our lives literally hung by the threads of red avalanche cords and by the ropes to which we were tied. It was March; snow cornices on the peaks, loosened by the warmth of the midday sun, broke off and roared down the mountain. In their descent they gathered momentum and volume and buried everything in their way. Hapless victims caught in an avalanche and buried under the heavy snow hardly ever escaped alive; their only chance for survival was for rescuers to trace them by the red cord and quickly dig them out.

On the crevasse-riddled glaciers we roped up in groups of three. There too the spring sun had softened snow bridges which hid deep ice cliffs going down hundreds of feet. Navigating in that territory was slow and cautious. Only one man (or woman) moved at a time while the two others on the rope belayed him. I was not there when the accident happened: the lead man, probing with his ski pole a suspicious looking patch of snow, fell into a crevasse fifteen feet down, until the rope tightened. There he hung, suspended, and unable to haul himself up by his own efforts. His two teammates could not move; they did not know whether the ground under their feet would hold, or whether they too would be hurled into the abyss. Nor could they leave and summon help. Darkness had fallen by the time the rescuers arrived; they lowered a flashlight to the man in the crevasse so that they could decide where to put ice anchors and ladders to descend and extricate the half-frozen victim. People who were on the scene later told us that the illumination of the glacier from below was the eeriest spectacle imaginable: the multiple reflections of the light from the blue cavern's crystalline walls seemed to come from a supernatural source. In the end, the victim was pulled to safety and carried down the mountain; he was lucky to have suffered nothing more serious than a few frozen toes.

This particular expedition was not organized by the Schiller School but by an expedition leader, a forerunner of the "Outward Bound" programs. He arranged adventurous outings all over the world; the announced purpose was to help individuals conquer fear and gain self-confidence. Years later there were stories that the real object of those excursions was to dispatch young people, ostensibly nature lovers, to foreign countries to collect secret military intelligence for the Fatherland. I did not know anything about a hidden agenda when I joined the group for those two weeks in Switzerland. Ever since I heard the rumors of espionage I kept wondering whether the man fell into the crevasse really by accident. Or was he looking for a munitions depot deep down in the glacier?

Whenever I returned home from one of those journeys, my mother reclaimed me as her property. A vacation away from home was simply a period of non-residence; whatever freedom I had enjoyed, whatever independence I had developed, all were combed out of the mental luggage I brought back with me. It was all for my own good, she indicated, and I believe that she meant well. But I was sixteen and resented not only the re-imposed constraints but her inability to understand the dynamics of my recent experiences.

What became a more effective detachment was the intellectual journey which I was about to begin. In the new school, history, philosophy, and literature were taught not as a rehash of textbook material, but as disciplines which required analytical thinking. It was taken for granted that we had read enough of Goethe and Schiller and that we were ready for non-conventional literature: the revolutionary Georg Buechner, Rilke, Thomas Mann, Ibsen, Wedekind, André Gide, Bernard Shaw, and Upton Sinclair. We were encouraged to delve into philosophy; I spent a happy year reading Schopenhauer and Nietzsche. Those of us who were not particularly attuned to poetry were taught how to appreciate both the form and substance of a poem. "Concentrate," said the teacher, and read us a modern poem—without mnemonic rhymes—two times in a row. After the second reading we were made to recite, word for word, what we had listened to. I still believe that this is the only method to commit anything to memory. The teachers were uncommonly devoted to their profession; many gave freely of their time after classes to teach a subject that was not in the official curriculum. To make us understand the intellectual climate of a historical period, one teacher whom I remember particularly made us listen to the music of those times. One series of lessons dealt with the structure of Bach's "Art of the Fugue"; another analyzed Wagner's opera cycle *The Ring of the Nibelungs*. But in spite of our teachers' labors, and labors of love, the Schiller Realgymnasium—its official name—did not rank first among the Frankfurt educational institutions. That place was reserved for the Lessing Gymnasium for boys, which was steeped in the traditional ideals of antiquity. Latin and Greek were obligatory. Had there been coeducation, my mother surely would have sent me to the Lessing Gymnasium. She much preferred its lofty ideals to the progressive—or as she often said, eccentric—principles of the Schiller School. The abstractions of the classic Greek tragedies were "safe." Modern drama raised too many iffy problems. My mother was not able to identify with, say, Ibsen's characters. The problems which agitated Hedda Gabler or the heroines of Bernard Shaw's plays had no relevance for her own tradition-based life; very reluctantly she admitted that she did not understand the new literature, and that she did not wish to understand it.

Unfortunately, science teaching in the Schiller School was decidedly inferior. The teachers, most of them with a Ph.D., had floundered on their way to becoming university professors and resented the ignominy of having to teach science to girls.

We had dancing lessons jointly with boys from a neighboring high school. The weekly events took place in the gym and were led by the gym teacher: "Now the gentlemen on this side of the hall step forward toward the ladies on the other side—slowly, no jostling, please, gentlemen!—each inviting his opposite to dance."

I went because everybody else went, but I disliked the whole thing, the sweaty smell of the adolescents, the monosyllables which they thought passed for conversation, and the boring long walk home in the enforced company of one's partner. Helene Mayer was lucky: Opel, the German automobile manufacturer, had rewarded her with a car for winning the Olympic gold medal. Now she could drive herself to and from parties to avoid, she said to us, all that inane chatter of her dance partners.

Taught by my mother that men were an—alas—inevitable evil, I misinterpreted their every word and gesture as either too forward or too dumb. Like most shy teenagers I was convinced that I was the most unpopular person in the world; the easiest remedy was to withdraw and withdraw I did. I went to parties anticipating that I would be a wallflower, and I probably was one more often than I want to remember.

A few years ago I met an old friend who reminisced about a party at the house of Hans Bethe, who later won a Nobel Prize in physics. "I remember that I took you as my date," he said, and went on to describe how Bethe, even then the inventive scientist, had devised a novel icebreaker: on arrival boys were to select a test tube from one rack, and girls from another one. Each of the tubes was filled with a different chemical. The idea was for a couple to pour portions of the contents into a petri dish and watch the outcome. If the two chemicals combined and formed a mixture, the boy-girl pair had "found each other." If not, they went to find a miscible combination with another partner. I have no memory of that event—parties were forgettable.

My mother took this all fairly seriously; eventually I would have to get married, and I could not afford to dismiss boys as dumbbells. I ought to go to every party to which I was invited instead of sitting and listening to the Floberts' radio in the evening. Radio—that ridiculous device invented for gullible low-class people, not for anybody who claimed to be educated. Our family did not get a radio until World War II. The Floberts owned a crystal set which had to be constantly adjusted. In the evening Uncle Albert and I flanked Aunt Flora, who was lying on her divan. Every few minutes we passed the earphones around. When Lindbergh flew the

Atlantic, we maintained continuity by hastily whispering a few keywords during the earphone exchange, being careful not to jolt the crystal lest we disrupt the sequence and miss a minute of that incredible story. Whenever I see Lindbergh's plane, the "Spirit of St. Louis," that poor little thing hanging down from the rafters in the Smithsonian, I get a jolt remembering the "real time" when it landed in Paris so many years ago. "I was there!"—I heard the shouting of the multitude.

I appreciated the tranquility at the Floberts' home. There were none of the wild outbursts to which my mother was given at unpredictable intervals. Aunt Flora did not want to fulfill her ambitions through me; she did not pressure me, and while she expressed a mild interest in what went on at school, she did not interfere with my going or coming as long as I checked in at the expected time. She accepted my school friends uncritically—with one exception. At lunch one day, I said that during gym that morning our teacher had taken us to swim in the Main River, and that we had a good time splashing around. "Poor Waltraut," I added, "missed a lot of fun. Her dermatologist had advised her that swimming in the undoubtedly polluted river would be bad for her complexion."

𝔐y aunt and uncle's forks and knives fell clattering onto the table. Waltraut was a "von," a member of an aristocratic family. I knew that the Floberts were quite impressed that she was in my class at school. "Waltraut said that?" they asked. "Incredible. What is the world coming to?" I had no idea what upset them—I had not said anything that could give offense. When I got home for the weekend, I asked my mother. "Of course they were upset," she said. "A young girl of a good family does not go to a dermatologist; dermatologists are only for people who have syphilis. Now, I don't think that Waltraut von G. went for a syphilis treatment, but that is the impression people get when you say the word 'dermatologist.' Do you know what syphilis is?" Not really—I knew the word because during his stay at a spa the past summer, my widowed grandfather had courted the widow of Paul Ehrlich, the famous discoverer of a treatment for syphilis. Whenever we met her in my grandfather's company, we had to curtsy.

"Let me enlighten you," continued my mother. "All men, your father, and Uncle Heinz, and Uncle Walter, and everybody, go to visit girls; and these girls have boyfriends, and when they get syphilis they give it to other people. If a man is rich enough, say, like Mr. N., he can afford to set those girls up so that they are there only for him and that reduces the risk of syphilis. So, now you know why the Floberts were stunned."

For me the explanation was not information but "noise" which I did not need to deal with. The reference to my father was probably one of the many accusations which my parents slung at each other through us children. Besides, I had no idea—nor was I interested—what my father and the other elderly men were doing when they visited "girls"—by definition women who were so much younger than they were. Sex was most definitely not a subject we schoolgirls were concerned with or talked about. For children "of good family" it did not exist until you were married. The village girls at the convent school said that the priest was the father, and some low-class girls the mothers, of the newborn babies found drowned in the village pond. Obviously, the girls were not "of good family," or they would not have behaved like animals. It was rumored that the high-school boys with whom we went to dances sometimes went to see low-class girls, but we were not really clear about what happened on those occasions. At fourteen, according to the guide at Goethe's birthplace in the Hirschgraben, Goethe had seduced Gretchen—an act which he expiated many years later in the drama *Faust*. We wondered whether our male contemporaries, in the spirit and flesh of Goethe, also seduced innocent young girls, or what did they do?

How could we know? When a young woman returned from her honeymoon, her unmarried women friends were not allowed to associate with her for several weeks—lest she tell them all about marital bliss.

Our ignorance was prodigious. One of my classmates, Magda, was a dwarfish, severely deformed girl who came from an old and highly respectable family. She was extremely bright, unassuming, and very popular. In her junior year at the Schiller School, she told her family at lunch one day about a composition the class had to write that morning. She was quite pleased with herself that she ended the paper with a suitable quote from Goethe. Which one, her father wanted to know. "A good f . . cking—that's what it takes to solve many a problem." "What did you say?" asked her father. Magda repeated. Mr. J. looked at Mrs. J., whose face had taken on a deep purple color. "Magda, do you realize what you wrote? Do you know what f . . cking is?" "Well," said Magda, "it's another word for proof—a sensible proof solves a problem. I thought it was a good ending. Or isn't it?" She looked with some concern at the stunned faces of her parents. "Oh, my poor child," exclaimed Mr. J., and then he and Mrs. J. told Magda the facts of life. But the calamity was not yet over. The paper had to be retrieved before the teacher read the incriminating sentence. "Where did the teacher put the papers after they were handed in?" "I think he took them to the office—he was going out of town tomorrow, he said." "Well, then there is hope. We have to go to the school and get your paper back. Quick, get your coat"; and off went Mr. J. and Magda. It was raining hard. Magda with her short legs had a hard time keeping up with her father, who was racing ahead. At a corner they collided with a family friend: "Why, Herr Obergerichtspraesident J.—where are you and young Magda rushing off to in this rainstorm?" "Just going for a little Spaziergang, for fresh air," said Mr. J. "Excuse us," and they pushed on. In no time at all they arrived at the school. Alas, it was locked; the janitor had gone home for the day. They scurried around the building, explored the yard in back, tried the cellar doors—no use. At last they found a partly opened window on the first floor, but unfortunately too high to reach. Mr. J. knelt down: "Get on my shoulders," he told Magda. "Perhaps you can grab the sill and pull yourself in." "If somebody sees us . . . ," said Magda. "But nobody is going to be outside in the driving rain; we have to give it a try." So they did. Magda got into the building, found her way to the office, grabbed her paper, and exited the same way.

I do not know how she substituted a cleansed version the next day. Of course, she told us all about her adventure. We thought it hilarious that the Herr Obergerichtspraesident—the highest ranking member of the judiciary—had been a party to breaking and entering. But that was only an incidental detail. "Magda," we beseeched her, "tell us, what *is* a f . . cking?"

So this is what people did when they were married.

A book proposing a trial marriage before a lifelong commitment had just been published in the United States and translated into German. It created a sensation and started a lot of talk on the subject. What seemed more important than the question of what happens to children born during a trial marriage was the fate of the bride's trousseau. Where would that go when the trial ended? In the Germany of my youth, no girl could be married before she and her fiancé had a complete set of household necessities, such as a non-negotiable quantity of bed, bath, table, and kitchen linen. My mother and each of her sisters started their married life with sets of blankets and featherbeds, at least twenty-four fine linen sheets and the same number of pillowcases, all hand embroidered and monogrammed, dozens of coarse sheets for the servants' beds, a banquet-sized tablecloth large enough for twenty-four diners, with two dozen matching napkins all monogrammed, a dozen smaller tablecloths and napkins, and so on. Not to mention silverware for twenty-four people, including oyster forks, berry spoons, an asparagus server, and heaven knows what else. A teaching assistant at the Schiller School once told us radiantly that she got two sheets as a Christmas present; now it would take her only two years to complete her trousseau. In two years she could get married! She had already been engaged for six years; neither she nor her fiancé—let alone the two sets of parents—would have thought it proper to start married life without the customary accoutrements. Can you imagine a young couple in their twenties sustaining a platonic love for eight years, walking arm in arm past shop windows, and murmuring to each other: "Only a dozen more tea towels, and then you'll be mine!"?

Marriage was the destiny for every girl. "When the time comes I'll do my best to marry you off to a man of culture," said my mother, "not to a dolt like your father. I'll pick a husband for you who is like Mr. O."—the husband of a much-envied school friend of hers. "Every single night after dinner he reads Goethe to Anneliese and the children. She tells me he is now on Volume 17." Since Goethe's collected works, including an abstruse discourse on the Theory of Color, comprised sixty volumes or more, I thought he'd still have a long way to go. "And on their twenty-fifth anniversary," continued my mother, "he is going to take Anneliese on a trip to Weimar, where Goethe spent most of his life. Imagine, they'll walk in Goethe's footsteps. But you should not have to wait that long to visit Weimar; you ought to go there for your honeymoon. I tell you what: I shall leave you and your husband alone for the first few days, and then I'll join you. I have always wanted to visit Weimar. Promise!" She took it for granted that her future son-in-law, whoever he might be, would be a man of culture, and therefore would enthusiastically embrace her plan for his—our—honeymoon in Weimar, that staid and unromantic small town.

Sometimes my mother's plans for my future extended beyond Frankfurt. "After your Abitur (the high-school graduation), I am going to send you to Paris, to be a trainee at the Rothschild's Bank. Then you can marry a Rothschild and . . ." "How would I ever meet one?" I asked. "Do you really think that they socialize with trainees?" "Of course, you can't attract a Rothschild or, for that matter, anybody, if you keep on being such a slob," said my mother angrily, sensing that perhaps her plan was not all that realistic. "Your stocking seams are always crooked, you have not the slightest flair for putting your hat on at the right angle. Look at cousin Anna— how chic she is! That's how you ought to look if you want to marry into the Rothschild family."

"I don't want to go to Paris," I said. "It's too far away." I did not want to add that working as a file clerk in a bank—or whatever else trainees do—was not a future I envisaged for myself. Most of all, I resented that I was not asked what I, Doris Schmitz, thought of the transaction. I would not let myself be sent away like a parcel with the destination printed on the outside. "You stupid ass," retorted my mother. "You are not being asked, you are told to do what I decide is in your own best interests. And don't forget, once you are married to a Rothschild, you can become a famous woman like Bertha von Suttner (the renowned pacifist of the pre-War years) or Sonja Kowalewska (a Russian mathematician whose biography my mother had just read) or Mme. Curie. Yes, be another Mme. Curie and invent radium! You will be famous!"

"But radium has already been discovered," I interjected. "Don't argue," said my mother, getting agitated. "You are going to invent radium or I'll pull your hair, you stupid ass, you blockhead. You are just being negative, like your father. You don't know the way the world works. I do. With the Rothschild connections you'll hear about all kinds of things that you can discover. And with their money they can easily finance you." She was convinced that with money and the right connections, everything was attainable: wealth, fame, passing of exams, winning the lottery, beating competitors, and making friends in the right places. Money and connections helped to avoid unpleasant things, such as service in the armed forces or lawsuits.

The only thing connections could not provide was good health. Illness was the result of stupidity or sinfulness, and therefore one did not talk about it. As late as 1960, my mother wrote in a letter that a mutual friend had a cataract operation. "But you must not mention it when you write her," my mother admonished me, adding, "I am sure she would not want anybody to know." Illness was almost always the punishment for "sinning," which was my mother's synonym for being sexually active and, by extension, for behaving stupidly in general, eating the wrong kind of food or dressing inappropriately for the prevailing outdoor temperature. It had nothing to do with the religious concept of sin. If our maid came down with a sore throat, it was probably because she had "sinned" with the milkman or the baker's boy who brought fresh rolls every morning for our breakfast.

Looking at ill health as a deplorable event that one is better off denying led my mother to treat the diseases of our childhood by herself rather than call in a physician when we came down with scarlet fever, measles, whooping cough, or chicken pox. Sometimes the results were near-fatal, but we survived. The physician made a serious face. "Frau Schmitz, the label on that bottle says that it is for external use only. And you made the children swallow that?" My mother tried to look innocent. "Well, Herr Doktor, I did not have the privilege of a medical education." Fundamentally she mistrusted physicians; she was not beyond stating that surgeons habitually cut holes into patients' bodies so that they can sew them up again. Before antibiotics, physicians were indeed quite ineffectual. "Dr. S. does not even know how to cure his asthma," said my mother. "How can he pretend to diagnose appendicitis? Dr. Y. cannot be trusted: his sister-in-law's daughter dates the son of the man who runs the restaurant at the railway depot. Trash! No Kultur!"

It puzzles me that I cannot remember how I and my schoolmates filled our time after school. None of us had a part-time job, not even babysitting. We had no chores to do at home. There was no TV to waste our time on, no malls to hang out at, no drugstore or ice-cream parlor where teenagers could meet. There was homework, of course, and piano practice. I was a fitness nut and spent a considerable amount of time on physical exercise: I went out for track at the local sports club, went swimming in the Main River in the summer, and skated on a frozen flooded field in the winter. Because our school did not have team sports, I joined a softball team of factory girls who practiced after work. So once a week or so I got on my bicycle and rode through the darkening streets to the industrial outskirts where the Frankfurt airport now stands. Surprisingly, the factory girls accepted me as a regular member, even though I was a highly privileged girl who, unlike them, did not have to toil on an assembly line. My mother probably thought that I was practicing with school friends. It never occurred to her that I was associating with "lower-class people," and I did not find it necessary to enlighten her.

Still, there must have been a lot of unaccounted-for time. What did we do? We walked a great deal. We walked across the bridge over the Main to our school on the opposite riverbank. We walked across the ice when the river froze solid during one very cold winter. We walked to carry messages to people who had no telephone. We walked to the municipal library to study. We walked all over town.

$\mathcal{T}$he city of Frankfurt which was rebuilt after the heavy bombing during World War II bears no resemblance to the pleasant, urbane, and handsome town in which I felt at home. Frankfurt had almost always been a self-governing "free city." Situated at the center of a network of trade routes, the city had never been invaded by an enemy, had never been under the sovereignty of a clerical or military overlord, except for a brief period of Prussian rule. Unhampered by the levies which overlords customarily imposed upon their subjects, the city became prosperous as a central market for goods and financial services. People said it was provincial compared to Berlin, the frenzied capital city of Germany. I would not have known. I had never been to Berlin. I liked Frankfurt the way it was. The moat beyond the old city walls had been transformed into a tree-lined esplanade. The half-timbered high-gabled houses in the medieval "old town" had been spruced up with colorful designs, and the stone towers which used to guard the city gates were made into apartments for resident artists. Above all, I savored the spirit of patrician enlightenment which connected the present to the past. The whole atmosphere was one of serene comfort and mercantile stability; there was no polluting industry nearby. There were no slums. The streets in the workingmen's district looked clean. There was an opera house, at least two municipal theaters, and half a dozen concert halls in which world-famous artists gave guest performances. My mother, who was very fond of the theater, often took me to shows. I remember vividly the famous Russian dancer Anna Pavlova in one of her last performances as "The Dying Swan," a moving apparition anticipating the end of her own life. Then there was the Israeli Habima theater's stunning performance of *The Golem*; the Don Cossack Choir; the brand-new and exciting *Beggars' Opera* by Kurt Weill; Carl Zuckmayer's *Captain of Koepenick*; and the premieres of compositions by Paul Hindemith, who lived in Frankfurt.

The high-school boy who frequently escorted me home from school—not because of a romantic attachment but because he lived in the neighborhood—was a member of the opera choir. The meager pay for his appearances as a spear carrier or a local yokel, depending on the opera, was supplemented by free tickets to the various performances. When his family did not want them, he gave them to me. I enjoyed being seated; my less lucky friends could afford only standing-room tickets.

Once in a great while there was a movie considered worth watching. Some have survived as classics: Fritz Lang's *Metropolis,* the early Charlie Chaplins, or *Saint Joan.* Juveniles were forbidden to watch *The Blue Angel* with Marlene Dietrich. We pulled our hats down over our foreheads and pretended to be over twenty-one. Our parents took a dim view of the movie version of *Faust.* A movie, a so-called art form that catered to the low tastes of the mob, was ipso facto a debasement of Goethe's sublime opus. Worse, how could the producer dare assign the role of Gretchen to a totally uneducated person, the daughter of our linen-mending seamstress? Her employers felt sorry for the poor woman whose daughter had gone astray and into movie acting. I saw the movie again last year. In fact, the actress was not bad at all.

✍ I had been at the Floberts for a year and a half when my mother had a falling out with them. I do not remember who started it or what it was about. Germans pride themselves on being truthful to a fault—no, I mean not "to" a fault, but truthful in telling others about their or their friends' or relatives' faults. Telling the truth was, and perhaps still is, a national virtue which elevates the worthy Germans above the insincere French, the hypocritical British, and the frivolous Italians. "I know the truth hurts," they will say, "but I tell you only for your own good . . ." And then they let go with whatever tactless criticism they can come up with. Aunt Flora as well as my mother were quite enamored of giving each other "a piece of my mind," about the other's appearance or ancestors or behavior. I guess one of those pieces was more jagged than the others and led to a temporary break-off of relations. The result was that I was promptly out-boarded and sent to live with the parents of two Schiller School alumnae.

It was quite unusual for people of high social standing to take in boarders. But Mr. R., who was a municipal judge, and his wife, who had been brought up in America, paid no attention to the status they were supposed to uphold. Having lost their savings during the inflation, they were determined not to vegetate in genteel poverty like most of their contemporaries. They took in boarders, so that they were able to stay on in their spacious house and enjoy many of the comforts they were used to. Mrs. R. was an energetic woman and made light of housing and feeding her paying guests. Besides myself there were two American girls who studied music at the nearby conservatory.

Recently, Mrs. R. had bought a washing machine. Nobody in her social circle had ever heard of such a contrivance. It created a sensation, although it was just a tub with an agitator and a pair of hand-fed wringers. People invited themselves to the house to watch Mrs. R. run the machine. For a lady to do the laundry was as eccentric as, say, climbing the Matterhorn. I cannot explain why it was considered so disreputable. Twenty-five years later, my mother was appalled when she visited us in the United States after World War II and saw me hanging clothes on the clothesline. "Good thing Aunt Flora is dead," she commented, "she'd never get over how you have come down in the world." Even my Vienna-born husband was shocked whenever he saw me ironing clothes. It hurt him, he said, to see his wife doing the lowest of all menial tasks. Could I not hire somebody to do it? Or at least, couldn't I iron when he was out of the house, or asleep at night?

※ While I was living at the R.'s, my grandfather Lahnstein fell ill and died. My mother inherited some money, with which she immediately bought a house in Frankfurt. We were going to move in right away, in time for the start of the new school year, especially because I was supposed to prepare for the finals. My mother threw herself immediately into negotiations with upholsterers, carpenters, and other craftsmen. With their help the unpretentious house became a comfortable home—at least for us, the masters. For the servants it was decidedly uncomfortable. With the kitchen in the basement, and just two large rooms to each of the three upstairs floors, there was no end to running up and down the stairs. Food and tableware rode on a dumbwaiter between the kitchen and the dining room on the first floor; but before, during, and after we ate, the servant ran up and down to load or unload the dumbwaiter and to serve at table.

The rooms had high ceilings and were well proportioned. There was a grand piano in the living room where my mother was now able to entertain her friends at tea. At last she was in a house of her own that was furnished with her own furniture—not with the Floberts' cast-off pieces, which we had been living with in Koenigstein. She used to stand behind the curtains looking out for us to come home from school. She was content, and we felt happy in the warmth of her welcome.

Unfortunately, her peace of mind did not last long.

My sister and I shared a bedroom on the third floor, next to the bedroom in which the maids slept. They let us hide love letters from our admirers in their keepsake boxes under their beds— mine in the cook's box, my sister's in the parlor maid's. We took the letters out at night and read them over and over again before we went to sleep. In the morning, before school, we hid them again. We were not about to stash them away in our room, where our mother regularly prowled through our belongings, trying to find I don't know what. She must have realized that we were hiding things from her, and she did not hesitate to break open locked bureau drawers. In the maids' room, we reasoned, the letters were likely to be safe; the maids' private lives did not count and were not worth spying on.

We tried to intercept the mailman before he got to our house, but with two and sometimes three daily mail deliveries, we did not always succeed. If he left letters addressed to us in the mailbox, the envelopes were often steamed open and resealed before we got to see them. Or else my mother insisted all day long that we show her what So-and-So had written, until, worn out by her unremitting pleading, we gave in.

It was assumed that youngsters who had advanced to the Abitur would go on to a university. For girls, the ostensible goal was continued education, but not a serious preparation for a professional future. Virtually every one of them expected to get married within three or four years, so that there really was no need to plan ahead. Still, women's emancipation was the coming thing, and people were more or less persuaded to let their daughters study at a university. They might even find a husband there; preferably one who would become a valuable assistant, perhaps a partner and a successor in the father's business or profession. In my case that was not an issue. My father's wholesale business was not worth preserving. However, for physicians or pharmacists who had no sons of their own, it was very important that a daughter marry a candidate able to step into the father's practice. Nobody thought of a daughter as her father's assistant or successor; the very idea portended the dreary prospect of spinsterhood for the girl. Until the thirties, the very few women who had become physicians, lawyers, or scientists—against fiendish opposition—were all unmarried. There may have been some exceptions, but I did not know of a single one. The social code of the bourgeois establishment not only denied a married woman's qualifications for a career but put real obstacles in her and her husband's way.

For my family—and I daresay for the vast majority of middle-class families—a university was terra incognita; they had only the vaguest idea of its structure and of the training for a profession.

None of the Lahnsteins, let alone the Schmitzes, had gone to a university; none of them had even finished high school. Like most people who did not have a higher education they were overawed by academicians. The Herr Professors and even the students were to them a superior species of mankind. It was not unusual for elderly ladies of my grandmother's generation to step off the sidewalk into the street—and into the path of oncoming horses—to give way to a group of whippersnapper "Herrn Studenten."

My parents knew only a handful of university-trained individuals who could have advised them; but the physicians thought of nothing but medicine, and the lawyers were focused on the law. Neither knew anything about other disciplines. Anyhow, my mother was not looking for advice; she knew how *she* wanted me to spend my years before marriage.

I wanted to study medicine. In Germany one went straight from high school into medical school or law school; students did not have the privilege—or durance vile, as you may put it—of spending four years on general subjects before concentrating on the field of their choice. Medicine would have been a good fit: the science aspect of a medical education would have satisfied my intellectual curiosity, and the practical approach to healing, my inclination toward hands-on applications. "Out of the question," said my mother. She cited the case of a medical student who was a very distant relative—a second cousin of a second cousin. One day that particular girl was studying in the library when a fellow student came along and wanted to talk to her. She buried her face in a book and told him to go away; she had to finish an assignment and did not want to be distracted. "This is typical behavior for girls in medical school," said my mother. "You would become just like what's her name, a man-hater who will never marry."

Her opposition was undoubtedly shored up by her mistrust of medicine and medicos. There was not going to be a compromise; she flatly ruled that I was not to study medicine. I could not defy her by getting a scholarship—I am not even sure that there were any for youngsters whose families were as well off as mine. Nor could I ask anybody else in the family for financial help; they would not have given me any against my mother's objections.

In retrospect, it all turned out for the best. Had I studied medicine it is unlikely that I would have met my husband and led such a happy and wonderful life with him.

If not medicine, then what? My fall-back option, chemistry or physics, was just as unacceptable. In vain did I remind my mother that not so long ago she had encouraged me, actually ordered me, to "invent radium like Mme. Curie." Why did she forbid me now to go in for science? "You forget the condition," she retorted. "I said: after you marry a Rothschild, not before. Mme. Curie was a genius, she did not have to marry rich, but you, who are obviously no genius, cannot afford to study science unless you are backed by a lot of money which you don't have at this stage. Get the idea out of your head."

There were no role models in Frankfurt—or for that matter, in Germany—to whom I could appeal; I did not know any woman scientist, and those of whom I had only heard or read were way down the ladder, professionally speaking. They were assistants-to, and unknown to the world outside the laboratories. A woman career counselor at the Schiller School predicted that if I chose to go into chemistry, I would be condemned to wash bottles for the rest of my life. As to physics—what a crazy idea! Einstein had published his great papers since 1904. Heisenberg and Schroedinger had laid the framework for quantum theory in the 1920s. But news of these discoveries had not yet reached the institutions of higher learning, let alone the high schools. In the United States, a professor of physics was an object of pity, lecturing on a moribund subject. In the state colleges he was said to rank just above the professor of meat-cutting. Dr. B., later president of New York University, once told me that in 1932 he had asked his thesis adviser to suggest a subject for his Ph.D. dissertation in physics. "Let me think," said the professor. "How about finding another decimal for pi?" Even erudite scientists in Europe thought that physics had come to a glorious end. An eminent German physicist, Max Born, declared in the late twenties that "in six months we will have (discovered) the proton, and physics as we know it will be over." In the unlikely event that my mother had relented, I would probably not have gone into a field which seemed to have no future.

I did not even suggest engineering; it was considered a very inferior subject in a society focused on the humanistic ideals; besides, women were not admitted to engineering courses. I knew that I did not want to study the soft sciences: history, literature, philosophy, psychology, or sociology. Nor zoology, botany, or biology, which at the time were largely descriptive or taxonomic. Nor religion or education. I knew I would be a very poor teacher.

It should have been obvious from the beginning that all these cogitations were irrelevant. My mother had made up her mind that I was going to study law. In the normal course of events I would soon be married and never practice what I studied. But still, one never knew. A lawyer, she assured me, has options: I could become a judge at a juvenile court or I could work in a publishing house. The latter was considered to be very desirable for educated ladies since it immersed them in the world of culture, intellect, and refinement, and not in mundane merchandise.

It was immaterial that I had not the slightest interest in the law; it was totally alien for me, and I rejected everything that had anything to do with it. I did not expect that I would ever be interested in it—and with that bias I never was. Still, it was the only choice. At least, I consoled myself, I was in good company. A hundred years before, Goethe had fallen in with some very shady characters, friends of Gretchen, who was a young waitress in a Frankfurt tavern. His father, on hearing of his son's involvement in those dubious affairs, ordered the young man immediately to leave town for Leipzig, a hundred miles away, where he was to study law. Goethe protested: he wanted to study the humanities. But his father, like my mother, laid down the law. The Law.

But first things first—and that meant becoming fluent in at least one foreign language. My mother and her sisters, like a good many other young girls from relatively well-off families, had been sent to finishing schools abroad after their last year in a girls' junior high. In those schools, in the French-speaking part of Switzerland or in England, the young ladies were taught social graces, along with French or English. There was still substantial emphasis on learning foreign languages in the 1920s. Out of thirty girls in my class, eight were sent abroad immediately upon graduation—

though not to boarding schools. By that time the German economy was in bad shape; our parents had suffered financial losses. We would have to defray at least part of the costs of living abroad by taking jobs as nannies, au pairs, or tutors. In our free time we were supposed to take courses at a university, preferably in the subjects we intended to pursue when we returned to Germany.

My mother decided that I was going to be an au pair in England. The London-based manager of one of Uncle Sigi's subsidiaries was mobilized to find a suitable family. He placed an ad on the front page of the *London Times*—the good old *Times*, with its four or five small-print columns of trivial personal and social announcements. Out of the half-dozen replies to the ad, one seemed interesting. A Mrs. Ffolkes-Brynn (those convoluted Old Family names!), in the south of England, wanted a German girl to tutor her eighteen-year-old daughter for the Cambridge entrance exam. The lady described herself as an Anglican and a widow who was well respected in the community. My father, as could be expected, said that woman was undoubtedly a White Slave Trader; nobody else would have such a virtuous identity. At my mother's urging, the London business manager went on an inspection tour; his report confirmed that the household was indeed very prim and proper, situated in the equally prim and proper town of Tunbridge Wells.

I hoped to leave right away, but for some reason my prospective hosts postponed my employment by six weeks. Having made no plans for such a delay, I was at loose ends. Not for long, though; my mother sent me to learn to sew—a craft she never mastered. Not a bad idea, except that its execution was somewhat bizarre. Only the most refined teaching environment would do, which meant a really ancient linen drapery shop. The establishment had an almost proprietary appointment as supplier of custom-tailored linens to all the aristocratic families in the state of Hessen-Nassau. There I was to spend the next six weeks as a volunteer apprentice. The first thing the needle workers taught me was to embroider crowns and florid monograms on the linen trousseau of a young countess. Thank goodness she rated only a three-point crown; for a duchess's trousseau I would have had to stitch another point, and for a princess still more. It was probably the most useless skill I ever acquired. I had just been "promoted" to French seams, a prerequisite for hand tailoring men's shirts, when the six weeks were over. Finally, I was off to England. Little did I know that within the next ten months I would live in four different sectors of English society—from the genteel formality of a Jane Austen type of country life to the twentieth-century slums of London. After an uneventful crossing I arrived at Dover, where the enormity of my adventure suddenly hit me: alone in a foreign country and left to my own skills, or lack of skills, in coping. The unfamiliar scent of British cigarettes, the biting mustard on the ham sandwich I bought at the station, and the tiny compartments of the train I was presently to board for Tunbridge Wells, combined to fill me with a foreboding of the strange place into which I had sauntered so lackadaisically.

TUNBRIDGE WELLS

I need not have worried: the environment I was about to enter was familiar; it was the England of the late nineteenth century, which we had read about in school. Tunbridge Wells was a watering place, a minor rival to Bath. People who took the cure paraded along the Pantiles, a columned passage around the springs. The social life consisted of church fairs, tombolas, and treasure hunts. As our friend reported, it was an ultra-respectable place, provincial and solid to the core, a century away from the irreverent London world of the between-the-wars generation of the Bright Young Things. Some of the male inhabitants went daily "up to London" to work in something vaguely identified as "the City." But, at least in the circles in which the Ffolkes-Brynns moved, most middle-aged people did not go to work at all; they lived comfortably off the fortune inherited from ancestors who had made it in the East India Company or another profitable overseas enterprise under the aegis of the British Empire, and of Her Majesty, our dear, late Queen Victoria. A thousand pounds a year or so provided a very good living. I never found out what the late Mr. Ffolkes-Brynn did during his lifetime. He had been Master of the Hounds at a local hunt, which was not a way to make money but to spend it, on horses and hounds, stable boys and trainers and keepers, not to mention the "bespoke," that is, custom-made gear for man and beast.

Concessions to the twentieth century did not clash with the eighteenth-century scenario. Mrs. Ffolkes-Brynn had a small car which she drove herself, and there was electricity in her thatched "cottage," actually a very adequate whitewashed house that was surrounded by a flower-filled garden.

The morning after my arrival I found mother and daughter and the maid on their knees in the breakfast room. I was invited to join them on the floor and, like them, to bury my face in the seat cushion of a chair. Mrs. Ffolkes-Brynn read a lesson from the Bible and led us in prayers, including a supplication for Divine Protection for me, the "stranger in our midst, so far from home." After that, the maid disappeared into the scullery, and the rest of us sat down to an ample breakfast of black tea, cold toast stacked in a silver rack, kippers, eggs, sausages—the works. Considering that the ladies hardly ever exerted themselves, I was amazed how much they ate in the course of a day. At eleven in the morning they refreshed themselves with tea and cookies. Tea was obligatory between lunch and dinner. Almost every day the maid baked muffins or scones and at least two different kinds of cakes to be consumed at tea time, plus two or three kinds of small sandwiches with cucumber or asparagus spears on soggy rounds of white bread. Dinner came a few hours later: meat, potatoes, and vegetables, and then a savory, which was followed by treacle tart or suet pudding. The only respite was on Sunday, when we dined on cold food in obeisance to Scripture: neither you nor your manservant or maidservant shall work on the Sabbath day.

Every single night we dressed in long evening gowns for dinner. Mrs. Ffolkes-Brynn also dressed elaborately for tea if she had friends in. She put on a hat to "pour" for the likewise hatted ladies who, in their full-flowered clothes, repeated the cabbage-rose pattern of the chintz-covered sofas.

In the mornings I tutored Agnes in speaking German and reading the assigned German books. One day Mrs. Ffolkes-Brynn asked my opinion about her daughter's progress. I praised Agnes's serious efforts but thought that she was not quite ready to read *Faust*, which was on the reading list. "What's *Faust?*" asked Mrs. Ffolkes-Brynn. "I expect it is a modern book—I never heard of it." I was speechless; was she joking? Little prig that I was, I simply could not imagine that there was anybody in God's wide world who did not know about Goethe's *Faust*—well, maybe some heathen tribes in Africa. But I was in a civilized place, and among people who had all the trappings of civilized beings. Catching myself, I began an outline of the plot, how Faust makes a pact with the devil and all the rest. When I came to Gretchen, Mrs. Ffolkes-Brynn showed a sign of recognition: "Oh, you mean 'Margarete,' the opera by Gounod! That must be it. I expect you call it *Faust* in Germany, but we British prefer the other name."

To cure my obvious ignorance she suggested that I read the books in her library, which consisted of a bookshelf outside the bathroom. It contained, among local trivia, the complete works of the prolific Baroness d'Orczy. I thanked her for her solicitude and took one after the other of those trashy backstairs romances into my room, pretending that I read and enjoyed them.

Not that there was much time for reading, except Sunday afternoons after church, when we were supposed to be quiet and occupy ourselves with edifying thoughts. Recreation on weekdays meant croquet or lawn tennis, shopping for expensively dowdy clothes, feminine chatter—lots of it—, visits to and from the ladies of the vicarage, and picnics. The young ladies' mothers chased the curate and other unmarried males with the usual determination. Regrettably, there was a shortage of young men. Traditionally, second sons—not to mention third or fourth sons—were sent "out" to India or Australia or another outpost of the Empire as soon as they had finished school. There was nothing to do for them in England. To be posted abroad was better than to be unemployed and penniless at home. Besides, distance from home and perhaps from undesirable companions was thought to build character, for young men as well as for young women. A girl in the Ffolkes-Brynns' circle who had fallen in love with a young Jew was promptly shipped off on a trip around the world to forget that really unsuitable attachment. A regular packet boat of the P. & O. Shipping Company took several weeks for the journey to Australia. But there were still a few three-masters around, big sailing frigates, which took twice as long. The unhappy girl was dispatched on one of those, in the special care of the captain. To while away the time, her mother had thoughtfully provided her with the Bible in Greek, which she was supposed to study, and ten pounds of knitting wool. Those appurtenances did not keep Agnes's friend from socializing with the crew and marrying the third mate as soon as the frigate reached Australia. Her parents admitted it was a dreadful mistake to have sent her on that journey—but then you cannot expect every radical cure to be effective.

The young men in their lonely outposts in Borneo or Tasmania or wherever tended to marry the nearest available female and to forget the girls at home with whom they had an "understanding." Agnes and her friends spent hours commenting on the fecklessness of those men, and of men in general, in the same manner of speech as the personae of Jane Austen's or Thackeray's novels of a hundred years ago. Sometimes I thought I could see Emma or Becky Sharp just skip around a corner and join us in High Street.

While I indulged in those flights of fancy, I was actually thrown out of the Ffolkes-Brynns' house in a way which paralleled poor Catherine Morland's expulsion from Northanger Abbey. The reason for my sudden dismissal was disingenuous, to say the least. Yes, I had been hired for three months' vacation until Agnes went up to Cambridge. But suddenly her mother had decided to take her to Switzerland for a month's vacation. Hence, I had to find another job.

Perhaps Mrs. Ffolkes-Brynn really had made a spur-of-the-moment decision. Perhaps I had unwittingly done something or forgot to do something for which she wanted to get rid of me. Perhaps her friends remonstrated with her for admitting me, a foreigner, into her house and their circle. England, and even more so Tunbridge Wells, were xenophobic to a degree. The French, the Italians, the Jews, and the Germans were all foreigners and inferiors, in spite of the Royal Family's provenance.

During World War II, it was reported that police told an elderly lady in Tunbridge Wells that she must, really must, draw her curtains at night for the blackout. On no condition must she let light shine out, because of the planes which rained bombs down at night. "What?" she was said to have replied. "Are you telling me that there are people flying through the air and throwing bombs at people's houses? I can't believe it—must be foreigners!"

I knew I had not thrown bombs, verbal or otherwise, but, nevertheless, I did not know what to do next. In that predicament, I agreed to Mrs. Ffolkes-Brynn's suggestion that I take an au pair job in a schoolteacher's family in the neighborhood. It was an abrupt step from the world of formal civility into one of Dickensian ill-tempered poverty. The impecunious schoolmaster, his harassed wife, and their many children lived a threadbare existence in a dilapidated and untidy house. They did not even have a single servant girl. If they had ever learned how to cope, they had forgotten it long ago. They just sat around and wrung their hands, reluctantly bestirring themselves to hustle up some food now and then. The youngsters with their runny noses and in their dirty clothes would have been certified as neglected children by any social worker who might have strayed into that house. I slept in a room with three of the girls, who hopped up and down on the beds and shrieked for an hour every night, claiming that bats had come into the room and nested in their hair. They would not go to sleep until I had combed through their matted hair and assured them that the bats were gone. In the daytime I was supposed to be a mother's helper, but in her worn-out state the poor woman was beyond giving directions on what to do next. The depressing atmosphere and the bad food were just about to get me down when, luckily, the stipulated time came to an end.

The new university semesters were about to begin, and so I went to London to look for a place to stay until I found another position. My mother had sent me the address of a boarding house which somebody had recommended. Not knowing any better place, I moved in. It was one of the hundreds of thousands of soot-covered row houses in the faceless and graceless gray streets of Finchley or Croydon. The establishment was run by a dour-faced woman. I would have been dour-faced too if fate had condemned me to become a boarding-house landlady. Her husband left every morning for the City, a black bowler hat on his head and an umbrella under his arm. At night, ten or so of us boarders gathered around the dining table and ate in silence whatever unlovely food the landlady dished out—usually Brussels sprouts and suet pudding. The conversation consisted of "would you kindly pass the salt?" or, if somebody was in an unusually communicative mood, "beastly weather today, isn't it?"

I had planned to register for courses at the University of London but found that only those students were admitted who intended to follow the regular four-year study plan. The admissions people suggested that I would be better off applying at the London School of Economics, a comparatively new and fully accredited institution which did not insist on the traditional four-year study commitment. I do not know whether the London School of Economics had been originally founded by the Fabians—an intellectually active branch of the early Socialists such as Sidney and Beatrice Webb, George Bernard Shaw, and their circle—or whether it owed its existence to the refusal of the old universities to teach economics. The Greek Classicist idea of a university did not consider economics part of the humanist disciplines. Long after the London School of Economics had been acclaimed as a first-rate institution, the Oxbridge dons only grudgingly admitted that it was probably an O.K. school for the lower classes who would not have gotten into Oxford or Cambridge anyhow.

Actually, the London School of Economics had an excellent reputation. It had a number of unusually stimulating teachers who attracted politically and socially aware students from all over the world. But when I wrote home that I was going to enroll there, I got a blistering letter back. My mother insisted that I MUST convince the University of London to let me register for just two semesters. I had graduated from a School, the Schiller School, I was not going to study at another "School," I belonged in a proper University. "So stop all this nonsense and go back to the University of London first thing tomorrow morning. This is an order." Many letters were sent back and forth until a compromise was reached. I must consult Uncle August on the subject, and we would abide by what he advised.

Uncle August was the brother of one of my grandmother's sisters-in-law who lived with his wife, Aunt Jenny, in a well-appointed house in Hampstead. They were a childless, elderly couple, kind people with whom I established a very close relationship from the moment I first called on them. Uncle August knew no more about the London School of Economics than the man-in-the-moon, but because he had made a substantial fortune in business, the family in Germany considered him to be an authority on everything. "Never heard of it," he said when I broached the subject. "It's in Aldwych, you said?" Yes, that's where the school was. "Hmph—there's a really rowdy music hall in the Aldwych; are you sure that's where you want to go? Tell you what, tomorrow morning I'll ring a chap—used to be in our office; now he works for another company at Kingsway at the bottom of Aldwych. I'll see what he says." The report must have been favorable because finally my mother gave in. I sent her the catalog as proof of the academic caliber of the school. It came back with checkmarks against eighteen courses for which I MUST register. An impossible assortment, chosen both for their presumable relevance for my professional future and because they filled all the daytime hours between nine and five.

Economics of Legal Rules and Institutions, Monetary Theory and the Banking System, International Business Transactions, Public Finance, Principles of Statistics, International Trade Theory, Business Cycles, Monetary Economics, Labor Economics, Monopoly and Competition, Government and Business, Social Theory and Comparative History, Economics and Society, History of Economics from the Roman Empire to the Industrial Revolution, the Origin of the Modern Economic System, and so on. My mother had no idea what university-level study meant; how could she have known? She did not realize that without any background I would have to start with Economics 101 just to keep my head above water. I wrote back saying as much but was overruled. I MUST register for all these courses; there was an inclusive fee. What a waste if I left something out. Even if I did not understand everything I must attend the classes—just listing the subjects on my record would look good on my future resumes.

Luckily, a foreign student's adviser in the admissions office caught the ridiculous list which I had dutifully written out and called me in. She listened to my explanation and cut the course number down to a manageable five. I must have come across as a singularly bewildered freshman, because she kept on asking why I had come to the London School of Economics, what my plans were and where I was staying. She listened with sympathy to my description of the dreary boarding house. If I remained in that place, she said, I would not learn the English language or anything about England or the British. How about moving into the University Women's Settlement House, where I would find congenial, educated women who by their example could show me how to lead a purposeful life? It would be an interesting experience and get me out of the stale anonymity of my current lodgings.

THE SETTLEMENT HOUSE

The welfare state of the past forty years has consigned settlement houses to oblivion. Even if they still exist at their old address, they are no longer centers of an important social movement. Today few people know what they once stood for. Before World War II, settlement houses were outposts in the slums where educated and socially concerned people lived among the poor. It is true that the dedication of the residents and their effective onslaughts against poverty and ignorance had a Lady Bountiful tinge. Nowadays we tend to scoff at top-down charity. But actually there was more to it than handing out alms. The Tunbridge Wells ladies prayed to save the souls and knitted woolen stockings to save the bodies of the heathens in far away Africa. In the settlements, there was an ongoing effort to build character, both in the rich and in the poor.

Settlement houses were started in London between 1870 and 1880 by a group of Oxford faculty members and students. Some of the founders were inspired by religious principles, especially Christian Socialist evangelism; others were motivated by concern about the havoc wrought by the Industrial Revolution. But whatever drove the founders, they all gave primacy to educating the poor—not just by transmitting formal knowledge, literature or arts, but by instilling in them the values and virtues of the upper class. Toynbee Hall in London's East End, named after an early enthusiastic supporter, the uncle of the latter-day historian, was the first settlement house; the University Women's Settlement came next. Both became models for similar institutions all over the world, such as the Henry Street Settlement in New York City and Hull House in Chicago, which was founded by Jane Addams.

The University Women's Settlement House stood in the slums of Southwark, an area which has since been razed to make room for the Royal Festival Hall and other public buildings. The outside of the house was nondescript. Inside, it was cheerfully comfortable. In the earlier years some settlement residents had traded creature comforts for the poor food and housing typical of the neighborhood. But the outburst of egalitarianism and self-denial did not last long, and the residents soon reverted to the life style to which they were accustomed. There was no point in denying profound inequalities among the population, but equality was not achieved by making the lives of the rich miserable. They—we— were ladies and gentlemen whose mission was to raise the standard of the poor, not to lower ours to their level. We did not talk to them in their coarse language or their Cockney accent; then why would it help anybody if we lived in misery? One of the recommendations of the founders was to avoid the imposition of impracticable schemes transplanted from a totally different social environment. Instead, priority should be given to satisfying the needs which the poor themselves identified. From the vantage point of the privileged, it seemed that with so many unmet needs, priorities did not matter. The criterion was real improvement over time. But the poor had their own value system. In one of the settlements in Whitechapel, in the heart of the East End, the people decided that self-improvement was a priority, right up there with better housing, better working conditions, better health care, and all the rest. The settlement responded with an adult education program that made great literature accessible to dockworkers, longshoremen, hod carriers, and the men who worked in the fish markets. Teaching was aural—the way we had learned poetry in the Schiller School. Few of the men knew how to read or write. Presentations of plays, stories, or poems were followed by discussions in which the men—there were no women—expressed their honest and distinctly unscholarly opinions. After a Shakespeare play, for instance, they argued that the wrong person got killed. "The other bloke should have been bumped off," and "If you had to live with a missus like that (Lady Macbeth, that is), you would have . . ." I suppose those men were more representative of the audience Shakespeare wrote for than the playgoers of our time.

At the University Women's Settlement, the objective was not self-improvement but housing and children's services. Like all the other residents I was required to put in a number of hours of social work each week. My assignment was to be a home visitor and to go from house to house to remind mothers to take their children to the free vaccination clinic. It was a shock to discover that at that time smallpox vaccinations were not compulsory in England. I do not recall which other specific vaccinations were being offered. The women were polite, even deferential. "Yes, Miss, I promise, I'll take Tommy, I'll take Minnie." Perhaps they really intended to. The squalor of the houses was heartbreaking; there were still lots of back-to-back houses. Rats ran up and down dank and stinking shafts. Broken stairs led to filthy upstairs rooms with shattered doors and boarded-up windows. How could people stand living in such dreadful conditions? Children and adults stared with vacant eyes at us well-intentioned visitors. What did we know of poverty and deprivation in our lives? We walked away from the mud in the streets and the dirty water in the gutter into our warm, well-lit, and comfortable settlement house.

Every afternoon the warden presided over tea in the drawing room with its lovely Queen Anne furniture. A silver tea service stood on a table next to the fireplace, where a cheery fire was kept going most of the time. Servants cooked and served our meals, cleaned our rooms, made the beds, and at night put heated bricks wrapped in towels under the bedcovers, to ward off the dampness that spread from the nearby Thames River. The neighborhood was grim and grimy; the factories along the riverbank discharged foul-smelling vapors over the blighted land. A greenish fog hovered over the dilapidated houses on the refuse-strewn streets, which seemed to stretch all the way to infinity.

Way back, Southwark had been a lively borough. The Globe Theatre of Shakespeare's time stood there; a 400-year-old tavern was still in business, pouring beer and ale in the old saloon. Its odd name, "The Elephant and Castle," was said to be a distortion of the original "Infanta of Castile." According to legend, a medieval procession carrying a Spanish Infanta who was betrothed to the son of an English King stopped at that tavern before crossing the river and entering the city proper.

The Old Vic Theatre was just around the corner from the settlement house. It stood in a street which was lined with hawkers' stalls. Its façade was almost indistinguishable from the squalid buildings left and right. But what glories inside! The Old Vic was as famous as a showcase for the great actors of the time as it was as a training academy for the aspiring young. I remember one resident telling us enthusiastically over supper about a new actor, a real comer, "Laurence Oliver or Olivet—you must go and see him in *Hamlet*."

We never worried about our safety when we walked day or night through the blighted district. The only people who groaned about our neighborhood were the young men who escorted us home after an evening out. They were not concerned about safety, though; they complained because by the time they had seen us home the streetcar had stopped running. It was a long trek on foot across the Thames bridge back to where they might find a bus or a subway to take them home.

The friendly settlement residents took me immediately under their wing. Some were teachers who were training social workers; others were students on long-term projects and assignments as part of their practice requirements. One who was a friend of Amelia Earhart used to take me to an airfield where we watched the great woman pilot practice takeoffs and landings. Amelia kept urging my friend to fly with her; she herself had taken up flying when a love affair broke up. My friend resisted; she had no such death wish—and airplanes being as rickety as they were in those days, she preferred to remain on the ground.

After I had been at the settlement for about a month, I was asked to take on an after-supper girls' club for young factory workers. I felt uncomfortable among those fifteen-year-olds who were stuck at a monotonous job for the past year or two and likely would remain there for the next thirty or forty years. If I remember, they were on an assembly line, filling face cream into little china jars. While I, so clearly advantaged, was free to explore a hundred different environments and possibilities. But the girls, far from resenting my obviously higher standing, welcomed me as somebody to lead them in games like musical chairs and pin-the-tail-on-the-donkey. They had had so little time and opportunity to be children.

It bothered me, and I am sure, some of the other residents as well, that the clubs and practically all the settlement services were set up only for those who had the drive and energy to improve themselves. The girls who came to the clubs were all "good" girls. The "bad" girls—the streetwalkers, the alcoholics, and all the other human wretches—were left for redemption by the Salvation Army. The ragged riffraff that lived next door was not our concern; we paid no attention to them, and they paid no attention to us. We did not even exist for them, as I learned later from one of those derelicts.

A FORMER THIEF

*B*y the time I met him he was an ex-derelict, and the occasion was a literary party in London's West End, where he and I were among the guests. A casual chat turned into a suggestion to have dinner together after the party. We sat down, the waitress came with the menus, and I was just about to decide what to order, when Moyshe Oyved (or Edwin Good as I knew him—not until later did I find out his real name) told me that I was going to feast on something far more glorious than restaurant fare. With that, he pulled a handful of pearls and loose gemstones out of a coat pocket and put them on my plate. "I always carry them with me," he said, as if that was the most usual thing to do. "And at night I plant them in the ground from where they rise and turn into the most beautiful stars in the sky." I did not ask how he dug them up the next morning; they did not look like glass beads which you can easily replace.

And then he told me his life story. His parents were desperately poor Russian Jews who, upon emigration to England, settled down in Whitechapel in London's East End. He grew up as a street urchin in tattered rags, begging and stealing apples and potatoes from the stalls of food vendors. Instead of going to school at age six, he was sent to a "fence" to learn how to pick pockets for silk handkerchiefs and watches. The fence attached a small bell to a man's coat and hung it on a hook on the wall. The young thieves-in-training had to snatch valuables from the coat's pockets without causing the bell to ring. When they had mastered that "art" they were sent out into the streets where the rich paraded about. "We did not go after you do-gooders," said my ex-derelict companion. "You did not have any of the shiny baubles that the fences can sell. You, in your sensible outfits with lisle stockings, darned lisle stockings at that, my God."

The thieves' world, as my dinner companion described it, was so much like the environment Dickens portrayed in *Oliver Twist,* I could hardly believe my ears. Hadn't we done away with that kind of lawlessness and brutality a hundred years ago? Now I learned that it was still rampant in my lifetime.

At one time, the watch stealer continued, he found himself with a pocket watch that was worthless because it had stopped running. He opened the back of the case, discovered the complicated mechanism inside, and somehow got the watch to run again. That led to a business of repairing whatever watches the young pickpockets brought in, which in turn led to a legitimate, or at least quasi-legitimate life. Step by step, he added rings, brooches, pendants, and necklaces to his inventory, and at last he became so successful that the Queen honored him by shopping at his store from time to time. He became well known in literary circles and in the art world; he wrote a book for which Jacob Epstein, the great sculptor, contributed a number of illustrations, and he obviously basked in the accolades of those whom he once stalked as potential victims.

Of course, I thought that the middle-aged little man, sitting across from me, had made up a good yarn. Who would have believed such an outrageous story? When we finished eating, he scooped up the jewels, put them back into his pockets and invited me to visit him sometime at his shop. Surprise! He really had told the truth about facts which could be checked, from which I deduced that he probably also had told the truth about his early years. Queen Mary had been seen to step out of her car and enter his shop, to the amazement of the shopkeepers next door, who could not understand what on earth Her Majesty saw in that dinky little Jew's store. Epstein had illustrated Moyshe's book—he gave me a copy. So, one day, I went to his shop. It was a treasure trove of barbaric and beautiful jewelry, large and rare stones in gold or silver settings which complemented each other. There were Mediterranean, Sephardic, and Egyptian designs of quite extraordinary style and workmanship. "Stand here," he commanded, and then he and one of his assistants decorated me—there is no other word for it—with those wonderful and expensive hangings, earrings, headbands, necklaces, bracelets, and rings. "Doesn't she look like the Queen of Sheba?" he asked the assistant. After a while I was being dismantled. "Enough for today," said Moyshe, "but any time you have a big date or an occasion where you want to look your best you can come and borrow all the jewelry you want. For free." It was hard to believe that the owner of those beautiful gems put such trust in my honesty. But he really meant it, and liberally lent me and other young women the most exquisite jewelry you can imagine.

We met a few more times for dinner. I was fascinated by a character who was so far out from anybody I had ever met; and he probably wanted somebody anonymous like me, to whom he could talk not only about his past but about his current concerns. A few years later, he went to live in Palestine before it became the state of Israel. He sent me a letter announcing the opening of his shop in Jerusalem with the logo: "Splendors of the Ages: Jewels and works of art from all generations for all generations specializing for collectors, children and fairies."

I had the good sense not to mention my strange new acquaintance in the letters I wrote home. Meeting for dinner with an ex-thief was plainly not a step up on the social ladder which the family in Frankfurt hoped I would climb. They were overjoyed when I reported that Aunt Jenny had invited me to a debutante ball she gave for one of her British nieces. A ball! A private ball at that! I would be in Society with a capital S! The party was better, and worse, than I anticipated. I looked presentable, thanks to Aunt Jenny, who lent me a ball gown. The kind soul even saw to it that my dance card was filled. But the young men were as dull as the high-school boys back home. They shuffled around the ballroom, hardly mumbling a word except "I say!" "You say—what?" No answer. At midnight supper I asked my table companion with forced brightness whether he did not agree that it was the most splendid party, etc. He leaned over to look at my name card: "Miss—err— Schmitz, I expect you don't go to many of these debutante parties?" "No." "Lucky you! Worst way to spend one's evenings." "Then why do you go?" "Because the mater makes me. See, all our mothers have gone to school together and they know what each of their respective offspring is worth and . . ."

"What do you mean—worth what?"

"Their worth: how much a dad has settled on a girl or how much a son can expect to inherit from an uncle—that's what determines who marries whom. Or rather, the mater decides."

In my letters home I described the ball as if I were a society-page reporter. I described the glamorous gowns and the flower-bedecked ballroom, but I left out my personal opinion and the comments of my table companion.

A description of another social event required even more creative writing—I could not possibly explain how I got drunk in the home of a titled couple.

My adviser at the London School of Economics sent me an invitation to spend a weekend at the country cottage of a Sir Fred and Lady Evelyn So-and-So, who belonged to some sort of a "Be Kind Toward Foreign Students" organization. The "cottage" and the whole establishment turned out to be far more elaborate than a fellow guest, a woman from Australia, and I had expected. A butler took my suitcase; a maid unpacked it and hung up my evening gown. Last year in Frankfurt it had seemed so stylish; here it looked deplorably inappropriate, but there was nothing I could do about it now. I went downstairs, where our hostess introduced us students to her other guests: Sir Hugh Camdiddle—"you have seen him in *Richard II* at the Willoughbrook Theatre, haven't you? Dame May Angleside, Lord Thingamabob, who is going to show us his hounds tomorrow." I was overawed; this was a unique opportunity to observe how the upper class lived. I must hang on every word, I told myself. But that turned out not to be easy. It was difficult to follow the mannered cadence of the gentry, the languid drawl of the men and the clipped chirping of the women. They tossed words around as if they were batting feather cocks. Occasionally somebody took notice of my presence. "So you come from Germany? Lovely country, all those cuckoo clocks." Our host was handing out small glasses which were filled with a colorless liquid. "Cocktail, Miss Schmitz?" Cocktails! How wicked! That was really sophistication. I had to pinch myself to make sure I was not dreaming. I had never tasted one. "Take it," urged my host, "it'll be good for you." I only remember taking one sip. It tasted strange. Immediately the room began to gyrate, the lights blurred, and I plopped down on the nearest seat, totally "out of it." I think I managed to get to the dining table when dinner was announced, but I have no recollection of the food or the talk which I had been so intent to commit to memory. I sat miserably and silently throughout the meal, afraid to open my mouth lest I say something totally inappropriate. Briefly, I thought of hiding out of sight under the table where I would wait for an opportunity to escape and make my way back to London during the night. That's how drunk I was.

The next morning I awoke in my bed when the maid came in. She drew the curtains back and put a tray with "an early cup of tea" next to my bed. She hoped that I had slept well and announced that she was now drawing my bath and breakfast was to be within an hour.

Somehow I made it through the day—a long brisk walk with the dogs, lunch at somebody else's house, and then the train ride back to London.

For weeks afterwards I indulged in morose self-incrimination. I had bungled a unique opportunity to listen to the undoubtedly sparkling dinner conversation of those glamorous individuals. Next time I would behave better—if I ever would have another chance.

My settlement friends, whom I told of my experience, made sympathetic noises. But underneath I sensed their distinct opinion that one should stay within the confinements of one's place in society. Nothing good came out of mixing with one's superiors. Their reaction was an almost identical replica of German middle-class doctrine.

By way of redemption for my deplorable behavior, I decided thenceforth to concentrate on my studies. It was hard going. Knowing nothing about economics, I found it difficult to follow the lectures. I read all the suggested textbooks to get a grip on the subject. In the library I struggled with Adam Smith and Malthus. The lack of precision in terminology bothered me no end. A "law" was supposed to be provable like a physical law, the law of gravity or Coulomb's law. How could the economists talk of a "law of diminishing returns"? What kind of a law was that? "Finance" was another puzzle. Take "money markets." A market was a place where you bought or sold things—produce or cattle or manufactured goods—for which you paid money. What do they sell in a money market? Money? And what do you pay for money? It made no sense whatsoever.

I suppose I would have been happier if the curriculum had included quantitative economics. However, before the thirties, economics was descriptive and vaguely theoretical. Once I had memorized the fundamentals I was on safe ground, without having to try and make sense of it. I took courses with Joan Robinson and Lionel Robbins. Both were excellent teachers, though not as entertaining, or as shallow, as Harold Laski, the much-admired left-wing labor theoretician. The students were a mixed lot, ranging from disheveled colonials to exquisitely turned-out British men and women.

Trying to sample different aspects of student life, I went out for hockey, but I was soon turned off by the Old Girls' boarding school whooping and their ridiculous outfits. I went "crewing" with a girls' team on the Serpentine, but that was not much fun either. Silent movies were just being replaced by "talkies." We students flocked to see—and hear—Al Jolson in *The Jazz Singer.* It was Kitsch, of course, but I was far from home and nobody ridiculed my low level of taste. And anyway, Kitsch in London seemed less objectionable than Kitsch in Frankfurt.

I went home for Christmas. Like any fledgling returning to the nest for the first time, I expected my family to be eager to hear of my adventures abroad. Father, Mother, and the siblings were at the railroad station to greet me. My brother handed me a bunch of flowers—an archaic German custom which I hope has been given up. The last thing a loaded-down traveler needs is to have to wrangle with a bouquet of fragile flowers. But once we got back to our house I was disappointed to discover that the family's agenda had priority. My stories would have to wait until after the holidays. The preparations for Christmas were in full swing; Lebkuchen, Pfeffernuesse, and Bethmaennchen, baked weeks earlier, were stashed away in tins to "ripen." Every day yet another cookie variety was added; dough was mixed, rolled out, baked, and decorated. In earlier years I had taken the traditional Christmas baking frenzy in my stride. Now I was in a rebellious mood: Christmas had lost its religious meaning, and I rejected all the "good will toward men" sentiments. I went to see my friends from school, whose homes were likewise suffused with the scents of baking and roasting. We talked of boys and studies and boys. I paid duty visits to the aunts and uncles. "How's England?" they asked, and "Did you meet a Lord? What was he like?" "He was quite old," I said, "about the age of my father." "Oh—did he have a son?" "I have no idea," I said. "Why do you ask?" "Well, he might have introduced you to his son, and, romance!" they winked. "The son might have fallen in love with you and, you know . . ." In their fantasy they saw themselves already related to a member of the aristocracy. With what relish would they refer to "my niece (cousin, second cousin, friend's daughter), Lady Doris, you know, the former Doris Schmitz."

My mother dismissed such speculations. Romance was stuff for novels or for the dreams of servant girls. Real people put money—or the lack of it—ahead of anything else. "Next year I am going to send you to Paris, where you can marry a Rothschild. They are so rich, they can afford to marry a girl who does not have money." She did not have the slightest doubt that I would go along with her idée fixe—rightly so. After all, I had been brought up to submit, with or without good grace, to her designs for my life. If I didn't, well . . .

Actually, I did receive a marriage proposal during those Christmas vacations. "Doris, there's a letter for you from Africa, from Africa—you hear!" cried my brother. "Are you pen pals with a Hottentot?" "Maybe with a Kaffir?" interjected my sister with a derogatory intonation. "Open it!" commanded my mother. A young Englishman with whom I had gone out a few times, before he was "sent out" to a posting abroad, wrote of his loneliness . . . "And when I return in three years on home leave, and if your heart is still free, my dearest Miss Doris, may I hope that you will accept me as your ever loving husband?"—a most decorous and stilted letter, probably copied from a Manual for Homesick Employees of H.M. Foreign Service. I had to laugh. "What's so funny?" asked my mother. "Can I read it too?" "Sure, I think you'll be amused." She was not—far from it. She flew into a rage. "How dare you!" "Dare what?" "Allow a man I don't know to propose marriage to you? Are you out of your mind? Who introduced him? Who is that Charlie? Did you ask him for references? Did you ask the warden to check him out?" My negative replies just fueled her fury. "You incompetent ass, you idiot, you dumb ox! Allowing some clown to propose marriage to you! If he had the slightest sense of propriety he would have come to us first. Obviously, he has something to hide. For all you know, his parents are divorced or his father has declared bankruptcy." I tried to convince my mother that I had no intention of marrying Charlie. Even if I had been in love with him, which I was not, I would not have wanted to become the wife of a foreign service officer in the bush in Africa, or in the marshes of the British West Indies, or wherever it would please His Majesty's Foreign Service to send him. The loneliness, the insistence on upholding British standards by dressing for dinner every night—never mind the climate or the bugs—were more than I wanted to put up with the rest of my life. All supplies would have to be shipped from England. "Please send me," I would write to the Army and Navy Stores in London, "please send me a case of tinned butter, applesauce, tea, stationery and pencils and a dinner dress, size whatever. My husband's service grade is #7 at Station No. 12348643." And good old Army and Navy would look up the rating of the post, who was my husband's superior officer, and how many subalterns served under him. Six months later, when the packet boat docked at the nearest port, my consignment would be transferred to a rickety railroad for the long trip into the interior, unloaded into a paddleboat, and finally carried on the shoulders of some sturdy natives to our bungalow. There I would unpack my new dinner dress, which was "different" by having fewer trimmings or less lace than the dress of the wife of my husband's superior, but more than what the wives of the subalterns rated.

No, thank you.

My mother did not listen. "You dumbbell—you did not even realize that Charlie was only after your money. Don't you know that all Englishmen go after American heiresses—hundreds, thousands of them? But I'll nip that idea of yours in the bud: I am going to disinherit you, and then where will you be?"

My mother was only forty-one years old at the time, and the prospect of being cut out of her will did not alarm me. Besides, there was no money to speak of. Nevertheless, my mother would raise the threat of disinheritance again and again in the future, whenever a young man, including my husband-to-be, showed an interest in me. After all, I was my mother's main emotional investment, and she was not going to allow it to be squandered on just any man. My failure to make a fairy-tale marriage would make her a failure and rob her life of any sense of achievement.

Not only was she going to cut me out of her will, she said. She had a far more severe punishment in store. An imbecile like me could not be allowed to be on her own. I was to stay in Frankfurt and live at home, where my goings and comings could be supervised. This very evening she was going to write to the settlement warden to ship my things back. That was a real blow. I cried and repented and finally won a small concession: I would be allowed to return to London and finish the spring term, on condition that I swore an oath to cut off all communications with Charlie, refuse to accept any letters he might have the audacity to send me, and, of course, never ever to see him again.

I swore: to be away from home was worth any oath.

Back in London I rushed to the aptly named Universal Aunts, an Employment Agency for Gentlewomen. I was determined to earn money and make myself financially independent. Never again would I knuckle under. Part-time work, babysitting or tutoring, could be fitted into my schedule at the university and the settlement.

"We may have just the right job for you," said one of the kindly Universal Aunts. "We have a request for an English-to-German translator for a professor from Hamburg who is here on a temporary research job. He was really looking for somebody who knows history and archaeology, but you might give it a try." I did—and I got the job.

The only way I can explain why I, an untrained economics freshman, was hired is that nobody else was available who had even my minimal qualifications: a fairly good knowledge of English and German, a decent grounding in art and history, and the willingness to work part-time for very little money. It was only after Hitler that exiled educated people began to move around Europe in search of whatever jobs were to be had. Up to that time the few young archaeologists or art historians who studied abroad were supported by grants; they would have considered it below their dignity to work as translators.

I had stumbled into the most fascinating job I ever had.

THE WARBURG INSTITUTE

$\mathcal{M}$y employer was Dr. Fritz Saxl, the Acting Director of the Warburg Institute in Hamburg. When I started to work for him, I did not have the vaguest idea of the Institute's pursuits. I did not know that it was then the foremost research institute in the world which specialized in tracing mankind's cultural lineage from the primitive to the current stage.

The Warburg Institute, which is now housed in a fairly inaccessible part of the Library of the British Museum in London, was established in the 1880s by Aby Warburg, an eccentric member of a distinguished banking family. The founder was interested not so much in the history of art as an aesthetic experience but as a history of images—of the projections developed by our ancestors as a defense against the uncontrollable forces of nature. Their gods, their heavens, their underworld, and their demons were the products of their image creation, their imagination.

The focus of Dr. Saxl's research in London was a Mithraic monument and the fight between chthonic and heavenly powers; my job was to translate a number of monographs from the English into German. The subject matter was difficult to understand; I did not even have the vocabulary. How did you spell "chthonic"? Dr. Saxl explained; he gave me books to read and patiently led me back through the ages to the creation myths of earliest man. He opened a door to knowledge of which I was totally ignorant. In the German humanistic tradition, art and history began in "historical" times. What cavemen did was inconsequential. Civilization and history progressed in lockstep from Mesopotamia to Egypt, to Hellenistic Greece, from the nomadic tribes of the Bible to Plato. Everything was strictly compartmentalized. Art was appreciated for its aesthetic content: harmony, form, color, or composition; I do not think that anybody ever told us that art was also a language of symbols which, like all languages, underwent numerous transformations over time. Such as, for example, the scene on a frieze on a pagan Roman sarcophagus which resurfaces, slightly changed, in a seventeenth-century Renaissance painting of the "Judgment of Paris" by Marcantonio Raimondi after Raphael. The very scene appears again—though with a different emphasis—in a painting by a French impressionist, Manet's *Déjeuner sur l'herbe,* in which a nude woman in the foreground has her back turned on two fully clothed men who seem to be engaged in an animated conversation between themselves without paying any attention to the beautiful woman.

The conventional explanation of the painting is that it exemplifies the impressionist style, particularly the transfer of an indoors subject—the painter and his model—to the liberating outdoors. Warburg traced the composition of the three figures back to what he called a "phobic engram," a projection of an image by which mankind tried to overcome the chaos and fear of the external world. In the sarcophagus, three river gods watch other gods go back to Olympus. In the Raphael painting, one of the river gods, a nymph, seems to be disinterested in the retreating gods and looks at the beholder, while her two companions look at the ascending gods. In the Manet picture the image is totally disconnected from any anthropomorphic meaning. Warburg even discovered a seventeenth-century Dutch painting with a bowdlerized version of the sarcophagus image. The composition of the three persons is similar to the previous representations, except that the object of their attention are cows in a pasture.

Under Saxl's guidance my introduction into the microcosm and macrocosm of ancient beliefs progressed at top speed. His work, according to his own description, was tilling the soil on the border-strip between art history, literature, science, and religion. Whenever I handed in a translation I was treated to a discourse on the subject matter. Unfortunately, I remember only a fraction of those interesting talks. For instance,

—that the propagation of the elaborate Egyptian cult of death was passed along to the Judaic and probably other Mideastern civilizations. A chariot of the Sun, the Pharaoh's vehicle for his return from the dead, was found in the Jewish Temple in Jerusalem, and Josiah ordered it to be burned (2 Kings 23:2).

—that the invention of myths as a defense put the gods into definable places in the sky: Jupiter, Mars, Venus, Saturn, and all the rest. This allowed man to overcome the chaos of a dangerous environment. And we still retain the names of those ancient gods!

—that the circumstance which led to the sublimation of the Christian sacrament for the burnt offerings of the Jewish rites was the destruction of the Temple in Jerusalem. Without a sanctuary it became impossible to continue the ceremonial sacrifice of animals on the altar. After a period of disuse, Christianity spiritualized the ancient rites by proclaiming the doctrine of God's sacrifice.

These and many other bewildering concepts had me question all my conventional ideas. It was an immensely gratifying experience. I know—now—that many of the Warburg-formulated models and deductions have been revised since the end of the twenties. They changed my perspective of the universe—something I had not much thought about during the last eight months. Or, more precisely, since I left the intellectually stimulating climate of the Schiller School. The atmosphere at the settlement house was decidedly non-U. My companions read Priestley's bland pastiches and Arnold Bennett's stories of the Midlands potteries. T. S. Eliot, Aldous Huxley, Evelyn Waugh, and Virginia Woolf were all but unknown to us; we knew the names of James Joyce and D. H. Lawrence only because of the publicity attending the banning of their books in England.

At the end of the spring term Saxl was going to return to Hamburg, and I to Frankfurt—not an alluring prospect. I handed in my last translation and sadly said goodbye, when my employer made an astonishing suggestion. "You don't seem to be enthusiastic about the law and economics, do you? But you seem to be very interested in the things the Warburg Institute is focused on. Why don't you switch over and study art and art history instead, here in London where you have the best teachers and resources? And another thing: we are thinking of working more closely with the British Museum and other London research institutions; you could be our part-time contact while you are at the university. We would pay you a small stipend, and, when you have your degree, you can work for us full time here or in Hamburg."

This was totally unexpected—way beyond anything I could hope for. My mother, I was sure, would be delighted. The Warburgs had an exceedingly high reputation—well, they were not the Rothschilds, but close. There were not many opportunities which could equal such an offer. I was wrong—once again. "You are going to come back and study law," wrote my mother. "That was the understanding when I sent you to England for two semesters. History of art—ridiculous! How will you ever earn a living? If and when the banker Warburgs are fed up with Aby's extravagances, they will refuse to finance the Institute—and then you'll be out of a job. Stop all that nonsense and prepare for your return."

I went back and registered at Frankfurt University for the prescribed law courses. Enrollment—at least in those days—meant payment of a fee and the signature of the professors at the start and the end of the term. To be admitted to the finals at the end of the four years' curriculum, one only had to show these signatures, but no proof that one had ever been to any of the classes. Some students did not even bother to obtain the signatures in person: they handed the forms and a tip to the janitor, who presented them to the professors. Nobody monitored attendance at classes. How students spent their time was their own business; they could loaf, drink beer, go fishing, or attend classes in any other field that seemed more interesting. Famous teachers at Frankfurt University, such as the theologian Paul Tillich or the sociologist Karl Mannheim, attracted large crowds; a specialist with a narrow field of interest might have two or three students at his lectures. I registered for the mandatory first-year courses: civil law, criminal law, and administrative law. The professors who taught the same subject year in and year out were bored and boring. I went to classes simply to get away from home. A fellow student whom I had known from the glacier ski trip was preparing for an explorer's adventure in the Russian Ural Mountains. Would I like to join the group? It was going to be a dangerous trip, physically as well as on account of the political risk. I was not tempted by that wild venture. At least I ought to learn Russian, he suggested, in case I changed my mind. So I joined him in Beginning Russian—I have forgotten everything since then except the Cyrillic alphabet.

Compared to the cosmopolitan students at the London School, the University of Frankfurt had a remarkably homogenous student body. The majority were, like me, the first in their families to attend a university and had to learn how to adapt. Without residence hall there was no social life comparable to American universities. One either lived at home or in a rented room. The young men had their fraternities, ranging from the high-status "dueling corps" down to more utilitarian associations. My friends and I pretended to ridicule the scar-faced corps members who so proudly exhibited the wounds they had collected on their archaic field of honor; but we would never admit how much we wanted them to ask us out on a date. How that would have raised our status!

Women, who had only recently been admitted to some—not all—academic courses, did not even have something like the men's societies. Their extracurricular activities were dating, politics, and sports, in that order.

A rather large proportion of all students, male and female, seemed to be hypnotized by the slogans of the political parties from the ultra Right to the ultra Left. The economic depression and the lack of any policy on the part of a weakened government had aggravated the tension between the extremists. Both the Nazis and the Communists competed relentlessly in recruiting members, especially among the gullible young people. The Communists had established a vociferous beachhead at the university's Institute for Social Research, which was for many years the leading intellectual think-tank of the Left. Its director, Max Horckheimer, presided over a circle of social philosophers including Theodore Adorno. It was financed by a well-known capitalist who took a cynical view of its function and output. "How can you, a millionaire, support a group that advocates expropriation of all private capital?" asked my mother. "Frau Schmitz," said the man, "you and your friends wouldn't raise an eyebrow if I chose to spend my money on keeping a stable of racehorses; as to myself, I find it more amusing to keep a stable of Communists."

Perhaps people like myself should have taken a greater part in politics, instead of leaving it to the hotheads on both sides. But I had no ambition to make soapbox speeches and considered it a waste of time to listen to somebody else's orations. Perhaps I could have become a good organizer—if anybody had enrolled me.

At the end of the semester my mother announced that she had arranged with a distant relative, a bank director, to take me on as an unpaid trainee during the summer vacations. The time spent on learning what banking was all about would stand me in good stead when I applied for a job at the Rothschild's Bank in Paris in the fall. And even if I did not get that job—considering the present bank crisis throughout Europe—a knowledge of finance would be most useful. Undoubtedly true—except that I did not acquire any knowledge of finance during my six-week stint. Given my ignorance and my distaste for the technicalities of banking, I did not profit in the least from handling letters of credit or discredit and the other arcane documents that blew in and out. I could not get over my amazement that people would chew their fingernails to the bone because some shares went up or down an eighth of one percent. What could one buy for that pitiful amount?

$\mathcal{A}$t last the vacations were over and I was packed off to Paris to study law, pending an improvement in the financial sector and an opening at the Rothschild's Bank. German law, like French law, was based on Roman law and the Code Napoleon. There was considerable similarity both in the systems and in the academic curriculums. German students taking law courses in France got credit in Germany in fulfillment of their total requirement for graduation. Thus, it made sense for me to enroll at the Sorbonne, and besides, I would learn French.

When she sent me to England, my mother had gone to great trouble to find a safe and reliable place for me to stay. A year later, satisfied that I had managed quite well in finding the University Women's Settlement, she did not give much thought to my prospective living arrangements in Paris. I had the address of a young woman from Frankfurt, a former fellow student, who had offered to put me up for a few days until I found my bearings. Edith, who was two years ahead of me, had left the university immediately after her father was forced to declare bankruptcy. That was a catastrophe which made his family outcasts overnight. Not one of her former friends would be seen in public in the company of the unfortunate wife; no man would ever consider marrying Edith, the daughter of a bankrupt businessman. Edith, who had been an exchange student in France during her high school years, went to Paris, where she found a job. According to what the family reported, it was a promising and well-paying job. Before the bankruptcy, Edith's mother had been on good terms with my mother's cousins, and in spite of the ostracism affecting her family, the good woman let it be known that Edith would be happy to have me stay with her until I was settled. An association with the daughter of a bankrupt man would have raised eyebrows in Frankfurt; it could be justified in Paris, where we knew no one anyway.

So, on arrival at the Gare du Nord, I took a taxi to Edith's place at the Place du Panthéon. There was a concierge at the entrance of the building, and a young man whom I asked to carry my steamer trunk to Mademoiselle V.'s apartment. In those days we always traveled with steamer trunks, unwieldy five-foot-high monsters which stood upright and opened like clam shells. They had hanging space for clothes and pull-out drawers for accessories, so that one did not have to unpack for months. They were incredibly heavy, and the young man was disinclined to lug it upstairs; of course there was no elevator. "Impossible," said the concierge, "there is no room for your big piece of luggage." "Ridiculous," I replied, "Mademoiselle has invited me to stay." The concierge shrugged her shoulders: "All right, see for yourself." I climbed up the stairs, the boy with the trunk right behind me. On the fourth floor he put the trunk down, knocked at a door, and hightailed it downstairs. The door opened to a narrow room, a bed on one side, a wardrobe on the other, and in the narrow passage between these objects stood a huge steamer trunk, a twin brother to mine. Edith and another young woman from Frankfurt sat on the bed. Each of them held a jelly glass that was half full with a clear liquid. "Come in and join us," they cried giddily. "Marion's beau brought a bottle of champagne and we are celebrating." They produced another empty jelly glass and we drank. I knew Marion only by her reputation—which was questionable, to put it charitably. "Sorry you can't stay here," said Edith. "Marion arrived ahead of you; and as you see, there is only one bed for the two of us. There is not even room for you to sleep on the floor."

A friend of my mother's had suggested that I rent a room in the apartment of one of the dozens of Russian princesses—real or fictitious—who had fled to Paris after the Russian Revolution. Unable to face the fact that their exile was going to be permanent, they clung to living in the manner to which they were accustomed, that is, in large apartments run by a bevy of servants. When the years went by and their money had dribbled away, they were forced to rent out rooms to strangers. I inspected a couple of those rooms or, shall we say, mausoleums, and left quickly. After a few days I found a room in a students' hotel close to Edith, who was then my only contact in all of France.

It was a curious beginning—very different from what I expected. Edith was not a piece of straight-laced Frankfurt transplanted, as it were, from there to here. She was not, as her mother had implied, a high-status administrator but the secretary-receptionist for a show-biz agent who booked oddities into nightclubs: sword-swallowers, dwarfs, ventriloquists, contortionists, and a horse that could add and subtract. It was her job to interview the queer fish and the freaks and to size up their entertainment value. "Did you count the performers in the flea circus before and after?" we asked her, "because I think I just saw one of them on your shirt collar."

I registered at the Sorbonne for law courses which fitted into my German curriculum. Theoretically, I could have benefited from listening to a different view of legal concepts; but in practice it was next to impossible for me to follow the drone of the teachers, the maîtres who talked so smoothly and so fast. My French was not good enough, the lecture halls were overcrowded, students were sitting on the floor and on the window sills. The noise and the heat produced by all those people were unbearable. I studied in the library—but Paris was beyond the dusty windows, and who wants to sit in a library over a legal text when everything invites, no, compels you to come out and enjoy?

Two weeks after my arrival, Uncle Sigi and a couple of his associates came to Paris for a business conference and a gay old time in which, or at least in some of which, they included me. We had dinner at the fanciest places. "Does Mademoiselle prefer the oysters No. 42 or 43?" asked the headwaiter, hovering over us. "What is the difference?" I asked. "Ah, Mademoiselle," in a tone that combined pity and condescension toward such a barbarian at the table, "there is a world of difference." "Well, then, I will have half a dozen of one and half a dozen of the other, perhaps I can tell afterwards." Of course I could not; I had no idea what oysters, any oysters, tasted like. After dinner we went to a cabaret or a glitzy show like the Folies Bergères or Josephine Baker with her banana tutu and all that. I caught Uncle Sigi watching me nervously out of the corner of his eye. He was embarrassed; he hoped that I, a *jeune fille,* would not "get" the innuendoes and the lascivious gestures. "Better not tell your mother that I brought you here," he said. I agreed—I was just as embarrassed.

Once he and his party left, my life rearranged itself in and around the Latin Quarter. There is no greater delight than to wake up in a strange city and be open to all sorts of adventures. For once I abandoned my anxious compulsion to conform to the Frankfurt norms of behavior. I could do whatever came into my head. I was free—I thought. Every morning I went down to the tavern around the corner for breakfast. People stood around the bar, which, like most Paris bars, had a large sink cover made of zinc. Workingmen quaffing a glass of brandy on their mid-morning break joined us late risers who had coffee and croissants. Those lovely warm croissants! I have not been able to recapture their taste anywhere, not even in Paris, on later visits.

The house in which I had rented a room was next to the Odéon theater and to Sylvia Beach's famous bookstore Shakespeare and Company. I peeked in and went out swiftly. Part of England, I thought, but I am here to learn about France. I was too benighted to appreciate the literary fame of the establishment in which a frail man with dark glasses—James Joyce—seemed to be a perennial fixture.

But this is not a travelogue, and I am not going to describe all my forays throughout the city and beyond. Most of the time I went by myself or with Marion; she had become a neophyte kept woman and was looking for diversions when her paramour was out of town. For a different type of company I went to the meetings of the German-French Students Association. Inspired by Romain Rolland, the advocate of pacifism, we trumpeted the No More War message—ineffectively, as it turned out. The association had a large contingent of Germans—I knew some of them from Frankfurt—and a minority of Frenchmen. It was practically impossible for me to find French students, male or female, to talk to; one told me candidly some time later that they could not figure me out—a young girl, unchaperoned and living by herself—what was I up to? In England I had no difficulty mixing with British people young and old, but I never established contact with the French throughout the two semesters I lived in Paris. I saw them only at a distance going about their business—housewives marketing at the small neighborhood stores, men carrying long loaves of fresh bread home for dinner, old ladies walking arm in arm in the parks, and the pretty young shop girls flitting through the street on their midday break. For my meals I went to cheap students' restaurants near the Sorbonne—I sat at the same table with my fellow students but no one ever spoke to me. We consumed the dreadful set-price menu in silence: an hors d'oeuvre of a small sad sardine on a tired lettuce leaf, a plate of French-fried potatoes, a greasy and shoe-leather-tough piece of steak—probably horsemeat—and a portion of sour red wine. It beats me how I stayed well and energetic on that diet for eight months—even at age nineteen there are limits to neglecting one's health.

One day a German student introduced me to a group of people at the Café du Dôme on Montparnasse. It was a motley bunch that was sitting outdoors around a large table. Some looked like paupers; I wondered what they were doing here. Their threadbare coats hung loosely around their starved bodies. Holes in their shoes were covered clumsily with plastic bandages. In today's vocabulary those people would have been labeled "The Homeless" and banned from a public café where well-to-do patrons congregated. My German companion told me that they were destitute artists, poets and painters who had not yet been "discovered." "Very interesting people," he added, "especially those two Dutchmen, Geer van Velde and his brother Bram." To me they looked like down-and-outers. I was, shall we say, flustered to sit among them. This was a social situation, not an uplifting session of the kind we had in the settlement in London, where we social workers mingled with the downtrodden to offer help and advice. Here I was, sitting with them as equals at a café terrace in Paris. What if a passer-by, an acquaintance from Frankfurt, saw me? I caught myself: don't be such a philistine—this is Paris, this is La Bohême, a new experience: go for it!

The tall one of the Dutch painters looked at me; he had an arresting, handsome face. Presently he got up and took a seat next to mine. I can't speak for him; for me it was love at first sight. I was smitten, infatuated—name any word you can think of. When I left a few hours later he asked me to come back the next day; he and his brother and their friends were going to be at the same location almost every evening. Well they might: it was a refuge from their miserable cold studios in the faraway outskirts of the city. At the Dôme, light and heat were free; you could sit all night next to a heater for the price of a cup of coffee and a roll.

The Dôme became my second home too. After dark I walked there, through the narrow twisting streets and past the railings of the Luxembourg Gardens up into the brightly glittering Boulevard Montparnasse. The company around the two brothers changed from day to day. Sometimes the tone was all frivolity and high camp; other evenings we sat almost wordlessly as in a trance. Whoever sold a painting or a story threw a party for everybody who happened to be at the table that night. We celebrated in dance halls, in nightclubs, and in the ateliers of fellow painters and sculptors. Next door to the Dôme was a gorgeous flower shop: the young hopefuls kept promising, "When I am famous I am going to buy out the shop, I am going to bring all of you armfuls of roses in the middle of winter." A young man walking on the Boulevard past our table and carrying one of those fantastic flower arrangements was rumored to be an American writer by the name of Hemingway. Somebody on the way up. Like his fellow Americans, he hung out at the Café de la Coupole across the street. We looked at them from a distance; we could never have afforded to share their expensive hard-drinking bouts. Fifty years later, when Geer had become a renowned painter and the subject of a biography, I read that the playwright Genet was a regular at our group. I do not remember; there were so many aspiring souls hanging out in the cafés. And anyway, I had eyes only for Geer.

To be young, to be in Paris, and to be in love is a cliché; I will not enlarge on it. Forgotten was the year in England, the settlement and the social conscience, the exalted erudition of the Warburg Institute, and, of course, my mother's orders to marry a Rothschild.

For Christmas Geer gave me a present: a portrait of myself. He was then in his Picassoesque phase, and the painting had all the edges and distortions of the master: one eye resting on the chin, the eyelashes next to the ear—it was hard enough to recognize the subject as the head of a woman, let alone to see any similarity with me. Still, I was proud of it; it was the most precious present he could afford, and it was a work of art. I took it home as such. My mother looked at it unenthusiastically—another piece of junk. But my father was furious. "Did you 'sit' for that painter?" "Yes." "In the nude?" "Of course not." I don't know whether he believed me. He had heard somewhere that *all* painters have nude models. "Makes no difference," he shouted, "he will put your head on the body of a nude and call it 'Doris Schmitz.' Shameful! It will hang in a gallery and everybody will think that you have become a fallen woman." I had to laugh; Geer's chances of having a painting accepted for an exhibition were beyond all reasonable expectations. He did not dare dream of such luck. I did not think it would ever happen. In all likelihood he would paint his heart out and die, without ever having found an appreciative public.

Disregarding my father's ranting I took the portrait away and put it in my room. When I came home the following summer it had disappeared. I do not know who threw it out. Too bad. Following those early hungry years, both van Veldes attained significant acclaim. One of Geer's fine paintings is in the Barnes Collection. Bram had many one-man exhibitions all over the world. A few years ago I passed through Paris on my way to Switzerland. To my surprise, I saw in a shop window a poster announcing a posthumous exhibition of Geer's works; he had died in the seventies. I went to see the paintings; they were quite different from what I had watched him paint so many years ago. A curator told me that they had become very valuable; the least expensive was priced at $40,000. And my portrait was in an ash can!

Once I got back to Paris after the Christmas vacations, I did not think about the future—or rather, I did not want to think about it. I loved being in love, and the delicious bittersweetness of knowing that there was no future for the two of us only added to my romantic enchantment. It was not that I did not trust my painter. I did not trust myself to remain with him forever. I looked at the tired, gray faces of other painters' wives. They were young women of my age who had prematurely grown old, loyally supporting their artist husbands in every way. They worked their fingers to the bone at menial jobs, cleaning houses and taking in washing—while the husbands sat in their studios or in coffeehouses, thinking high-minded thoughts or taking up with pretty young things. How much faith did it take for a wife to believe in her man's genius? Did she never ask herself whether her sacrifices were worthwhile? Would she turn into a nagging shrew when she and her man grew old, forty or fifty, and still unappreciated by the world?

Would I want to become one of them? Certainly not. "I don't see you marrying a solid German bourgeois either," said Geer, "or how do you see yourself ten years from now?" Not as a hausfrau, I was sure, drooling over my grandmother's monogrammed linen that my mother was saving for me. But neither did I see myself spending the rest of my life in rags.

For now I decided to put all those problems aside and hold on to the unalloyed happiness of today and tomorrow and the days after. There were still three months left before I had to return to Germany: half of January, all of February and March, and half of April. Three months in paradise!

By March the time seemed to have become terrifyingly short. I began to look for a job which would enable me to stay on, even if my mother disinherited me. During the winter I had done some temporary work as a translator or, with Marion, as a travel aide on the autobuses which drove German tourists through Paris. My wages went for fripperies: little nothings of a hat, a piece of veil and a bunch of flowers, elbow-length black vampish gloves— things which the French are so good at whipping up. They would, I hoped, compensate for the dullness of my German outfits. But what I earned that way was pocket money; I could not possibly live on it. Somebody told me that Wanda Landowska, the great harpsichord musician, was looking for a multilingual assistant. I applied for the job at once. To my surprise I received an invitation to come for an interview. "Watch out," said Geer, "it is a lesbian establishment; she has ruined more girls than one." "Don't worry," I said, "you know that isn't my line at all." So, one fine Sunday spring morning I traveled to Madame's house in Fontainebleau, outside of Paris, to present myself. It was an impressive establishment in a lovely park with tall leafy trees. Inside I was handed from one young woman attendant to another; they all looked alike in long plain gowns which were girded, like monks' robes, with thick plaited cords. Had they stood next to each other, they would have looked like a chorus of priestesses in a Greek drama. Finally I came into Madame's presence. She looked me over, asked a few unimportant questions, and decided on the spot that I would do, and how soon could I start? Whereupon I was ushered out as ceremoniously as I had been ushered in. The whole scene, I had to admit, made me feel somewhat uneasy, but the job seemed to be too good to be true; I would not have to return to Germany; I would be staying in France near Geer. In my letters home I stressed the great opportunity the job offered, the great music I would be able to hear, the travels and the chances to meet virtually all the famous performers and conductors in the world. An alarmed letter arrived by return mail. For heaven's sake—you must not, repeat not, take that job under any circumstances: Landowska is a well-known lesbian.

The following day Geer came up with another suggestion: "Don't go back. Come with us to Corsica. Bram and I are going; one can live there for practically nothing. Just think of the luminous light in the Mediterranean climate and what it will do for our painting. Don't go back to Germany." Corsica! The island had not yet become a target for tourists. Did anybody know how to get there and, more important, how to get back? I knew that Napoleon had managed to leave Corsica, his birthplace, for fame and fortune in France. But how would I be able to get back in case I did not like it? The painters would be happy painting all day; there was nothing for me to do there. In a few months, perhaps sooner, I would be fed up loafing around. And then what?

The semester ended, the chestnut trees were in bloom, and

lovers strolled along the Seine. Paris was at its loveliest. The time had come to let go. I never saw Geer again, never wrote him, never heard from him again.

Anybody could have pointed out that I had just spent the best part of a year bumming around. My French had become fluent, but my nominal law studies had been put on the back burner. I had not learned anything useful; I had not contributed anything whatsoever to society. There was a lot of catching up to do. I was not rushing into that, though, when I arrived back home. For weeks I indulged in grieving for my lost love. I tormented myself asking whether I had made the right decision. Nobody had ever suffered such heartache I was sure.

I must have been an unbearably weepy young woman; and understandably, my mother did not feel like dealing with my gloomy moroseness. She suggested that I leave and study someplace away from Frankfurt for the next semester.

*I*n the halcyon days before overcrowding had begun, German students were allowed, even encouraged, to study at diverse universities, in the tradition of the medieval scholars who followed their teachers and masters from one monastery to another. Freedom of movement was a self-evident entitlement up to the later semesters and before the finals. The uniformity of the syllabus throughout Germany made it possible to study anywhere, so that the students did not have to make any academic adjustments. They could follow a regular study plan wherever they chose to be. Thus they moved around for all kinds of reasons. The universities of Munich and Innsbruck were favorite destinations for the winter semesters because they offered ample opportunities for skiing. In the summer Hamburg or Kiel attracted those who liked saltwater sailing. Many students opted to spend a semester or two at universities which emphasized special disciplines: Goettingen for math students, Marburg for theologians, and Heidelberg for philosophers.

My mother suggested Kiel, a quiet town on the Baltic. The university there had a good reputation, and the city of Kiel supposedly had an innocuous provincial ambience. Formerly the seaport of the Imperial German Navy, it had become an unimportant backwater when the navy was reduced to a shadow of its former glory under the Treaty of Versailles. The retired admirals and captains and their widows still hung around, remembering when. One could be quite sure that neither the city nor the university offered any diversions which could possibly distract me from making up what I had so badly neglected in Paris. The law faculty and the number of law students was fairly small; everybody took his or her studies very seriously, and so did I. Sailing was the big thing, or rather, the only thing to do. Having been born and raised inland, I had not developed any affinity for the sport. I thought that sailing could be a challenge for someone who is in charge. For a landlubber like me it was a dismal bore to be just a passenger. I declined without regret the invitations of well-meaning boatmen. It was much more rewarding to wander inland through the summery small-scale landscape of Schleswig-Holstein. Flowers bloomed abundantly in fields and meadows, and the hedges surrounding the many little lakes were full of sweet-smelling hedgeroses.

At the end of the semester, I returned to Frankfurt, determined to throw myself at The Law. I wanted to get it over with as fast as possible. The university's graduation exam corresponded to the bar exam. The J.D., optional but desirable, could be pursued simultaneously or later. I decided to start at once on my Ph.D. thesis and to schedule both exams in close succession, so I would have to cram only once for both. Given my lengthy sojourns abroad, a subject in international law was the obvious choice. If I remember, it had something to do with the law of the sea. A professor who specialized in international law allowed me to attend his weekly seminar which was normally open only to more advanced students. He conducted the seminar at his house after dinner. Or rather, he did not conduct; he just sat by and listened while two extremely eloquent young men took over the proceedings: Fritz Kraemer, a German, and Peter Drucker, an Austrian. Those two argued endlessly about all kinds of issues in international law, hardly ever letting anybody else get a word in edgewise. Fritz affected the style and manners of an aristocrat of the Kaiser years. Disregarding the red-black-gold flag of the Weimar Republic, he insisted on the colors of the Hohenzollern time. Students stood on the bridge across the Main to watch—and jeer at him—when he sailed past in his little foldboat, wearing nothing but bathing trunks and a monocle in one eye and flying the black-white-red flag of the Kaiser's Empire. In class, the legal aspects of this incongruity were debated with great ponderation. Did the law of the sea apply to foldboats? Spirited arguments invariably extended beyond the end of the evening; when we walked homewards, Drucker and Kraemer kept on talking to each other as if I, between the two of them, was a nonperson. Much later they told me they were in awe of me because I never opened my mouth; they thought I disdained to participate in a conversation which I considered below my level of competence. Ah well . . .

I had also enrolled in a class on constitutional law taught by the same professor, who was a seasoned hypochondriac. Feeling unwell one day, he delegated Peter Drucker to take over. Peter was unprepared, of course. So, instead of a classroom lecture, he announced, we would go to the City Museum and study the symbols of our constitutional history: the crowns, scepters, and orbs and parchments declaring peace; documents declaring war are usually not shown to the public. We would see all the celebrated trappings that were said to have led us from the dark into the modern, enlightened days.

Unlike the standard historical depositories, Frankfurt's City Museum was housed in a magnificent mansion called the "Roemer." Since 867 its grand hall was the scene where the Prince Electors convened to vote on the next Emperor of the Holy Roman Empire. After they had made their choice, the nominated ruler-to-be went out onto a balcony to show himself to his people, who were assembled in the square below. Shortly after, he was led in a procession through a short cobblestone passage to the nearby church, the Dom, where the ceremonial election and the coronation took place. A large fountain stood in the center of the Roemer Square, which was probably the most perfectly proportioned square in all of Germany. It was surrounded by richly decorated old patrician houses. Their old names were displayed on iron signs:

House of the Angel, House of the Golden Griffon, House of the Wild Man. I liked that part of the city better than any other section.

Having seen the museum exhibits several times in the past, I went to a window and looked at the picturesque scene outside, when I heard Mr. Drucker call it quits for the day. We started to descend the broad stone stairs, which were worn away by the footsteps of countless temporal and spiritual dignitaries. Mr. Drucker sidled toward me, and by the time we had walked down all the way he had asked where I was going to have lunch. "At home, of course." "Oh." He seemed to hesitate—"I thought we could have lunch together." "We can," I said, "but I have to telephone home not to expect me." He suggested a vegetarian restaurant nearby—I remember the food was terrible, but the conversation was interesting. Mr. Drucker told me that he was the Foreign Editor of a large Frankfurt daily newspaper, the *General Anzeiger,* and that he was working toward his J. D. on the side. All high-minded people, and the bona fide members of the Frankfurt intelligentsia, subscribed to or at least read another daily, the *Frankfurter Zeitung,* which was synonymous with political wisdom and Kultur; but they also subscribed to the middle-brow—and more lively—*General Anzeiger*—"for the servants, you know." Of course, the master and the mistress read every issue before they sent it out to the kitchen. Asked at dinner where and with whom I had lunch, I told the family that my companion worked at the *General Anzeiger* while completing his law studies. "What does he do at the paper?" asked my mother. "Is he a copy boy or what?" "No, he is the Foreign Editor." "That's what he told you to impress you," said my mother. "Do you really believe the General Anzeiger would hire a snot-nosed twenty-three year old as their Foreign Editor?" "He really is," I replied. "Here." I showed her the day's paper. "See, here are his initials, P. F. D." My mother became irate. "Do you mean to say that I have been taken in by a greenhorn, that I have swallowed for years the so-called opinions of a boy who is not yet dry behind his ears? That is outright deception on the part of the paper." She went to the telephone and cancelled her subscription to the *General Anzeiger* forthwith.

After that initial lunch, Peter Drucker and I went out on a few casual dates, but our interest in one another never developed into a serious, or even unserious, attachment. My mother was relieved—she certainly did not want me to get involved with an Austrian—proverbially frivolous and irresponsible people, given to playing schmaltzy tunes on the violin. "You mix them up with gypsies," I said. "I like Austrians." "I'll never permit you to marry an Austrian!" said my mother. "They have no sense for the seriousness of life." Still, Drucker had a job which gave him an entrée to important people to whom he might conceivably introduce me. In that case I would have to be better dressed. My mother took me to the most fashionable store in Frankfurt and bought me a very elegant outfit—the first ready-made dress I ever had.

I did not have a chance to wear it often. In the depressing political and economic atmosphere that hung over Germany, there were few occasions for social entertainment. The Communists, under orders by Stalin, attacked the Social Democrats from the Left; the Nazis, rumored to be financed also by the Soviets, attacked from the Right. The middle class, which used to be the mainstay of the Center parties, had been badly decimated by the disastrous inflation of the early twenties. Ten years later it did not have the strength to resist the pressures from either side. A series of political scandals fueled the general discontent. There was large-scale unemployment, and nobody had any ideas how to brake the rapid descent into chaos. The average citizens nodded their heads and acquiesced in the bourgeois slumber which our great poets had already deplored a hundred years ago. Prominent people who previously had adopted a lofty attitude toward politics now identified with Communists or Nazis with the justification, "Let's see what the Extremists can do." A great many people did not believe that the Nazis, if they prevailed, would really carry out the program Hitler had outlined in *Mein Kampf.* Surely, President Hindenburg would not allow it. They would just form a government like all the others. Elli, a childhood friend from Koenigstein who was engaged to a Storm Trooper, assured me that nothing was going to happen; it was all election rhetoric. Against all evidence many Jews, especially the assimilated ones, did not believe that they would be in serious trouble as long as they adopted a low profile until the Nazi tornado had passed over. The orthodox Jews had a more realistic vision: they studied vernacular Hebrew and prepared to emigrate to Palestine. Klaus Mann, exiled from Germany with Thomas Mann, his famous father, wrote several years later that "the vast majority of the Jews would have remained in the Reich if only the Nazis had allowed them to stay. There is nothing derogatory or malicious about this statement. Why would the Jewish sector of the German bourgeoisie have protested against the government that was hailed or at least accepted by millions of their non-Jewish countrymen?"

This is all moot now. The Holocaust stays in our collective memory. Nobody anticipated it as late as 1931. We students worried about the looming bar exam, about jobs and one's popularity with the opposite sex—the usual. A good many of our contemporaries participated in the ubiquitous political rallies where protesters and hecklers were badly beaten up. But for most of us life went on as usual.

My mother sent me to Nuernberg on a mission to her sister Margret—I really cannot remember what it was about. The only memorable thing about the trip was that I came back by plane. The government, anxious to popularize travel by air, offered students a very low fare. So, why shouldn't I be enterprising? It was quite an adventurous undertaking, considering that civilian air travel was still in its infancy. The little bi-plane flew at low altitude, where it was tossed around by the updrafts from the Spessart mountains. On my return I was hailed as a daredevil. I had been the first one in our family and our circle of acquaintances to have flown in a plane.

When I left Frankfurt for Holland in the summer of 1932, Peter Drucker was out of my life. We had drifted so far apart that I did not even say goodbye to him. How we found each other again is another story.

Let me pass over the year I spent in Holland—probably the most frustrating time of my life. The job in our Dutch friend's shipping company was deadly dull. The grey skies and the persistent fog and rain put me in bad humor most of the time. Once I had finished my J.D. thesis, there was no reason why I should stay on. In the meantime, Hitler had officially taken over in Germany; I was not going to go back for a useless law degree. There was no longer the traditional German Civil Law; it had been replaced by the Nationalsocialist Law—whatever that meant. Lawyers were being reeducated in boot camps. But I would not have been allowed to practice law anyhow because of my Jewish ancestors.

Taking advantage of a long weekend, I went to London looking for a job and an opportunity to get out of Holland. It did not take me long to get an offer: Mr. Barnes, a distinguished professor of international law, was looking for a research assistant. Pay was to be in kind: room and board in the pleasant house he shared with his wife. I accepted on the spot; in a week or two I had moved to London. The Barneses were exceedingly kind people who treated me as a member of their family.

One day, riding down the very long escalator in the Piccadilly Underground station, I was hailed by somebody who was riding up on the complementary escalator on the other side of the wide hall. It was Peter Drucker. We waved at each other, and as soon as he came to the top he turned around to ride down to meet me, while I turned around at the bottom and rode up to meet him. After we had played that game one more time, one of us—I forget who—used his or her head and waited for the other. We went to a restaurant and talked. Peter had lost his job at the *General Anzeiger* and, with it, the prospects for a promising future in Germany. Now he was in London working for an insurance company. Both of us were lucky to have found jobs at all at a time of high unemployment.

Peter and I were happy to have met again so fortuitously. Both of us had been cut off from our moorings, Peter more than I who was still nominally a student. Having lived in England before, I was quite fluent in English. For Peter, England was largely terra incognita. Both of us were lonely in an essentially xenophobic environment. We were in despair over the worsening situation in

Germany—and frightened by the apathy and the unwillingness of the British to see through Hitler's dangerous game plan. So, drawn together by shared apprehensions, Peter and I resumed our companionable relationship from the Frankfurt days.

Word must have gotten to Vienna that Peter was dating a German girl. Horrors—a German girl as a future daughter-in-law was as unacceptable to Mrs. Drucker as was the prospect of an Austrian son-in-law to Mrs. Schmitz. It was like suggesting a union between a Yankee and a member of an old Southern family. Worse: the German girl had no money. Just as my mother was determined that I marry a Rothschild, so Peter's mother was determined that he marry "a Sassoon," a member of an immensely wealthy British family. In both cases these were pipe dreams; but the immediate task was to tear Peter away from That German Girl. Mrs. Drucker at once dispatched a Viennese girl, a childhood friend of Peter's, to London with orders to captivate him. Peter felt he had to show Maria around, which did not sit well with me. I quid-pro-quo'ed, and by the time she went back home, our romance had waned. It kept on waxing and waning over the next couple of months; neither of us thought that it would continue for long.

A few months after my arrival, the Barneses went to the United States on a lecture tour and asked me to house-sit for them during their absence. Their house stood in a dell, called the Vale of Health, in the middle of the vast, grassy Hampstead Heath. There were a few more houses nearby, all of which had been built by and for artists some fifty or sixty years before. In that rural enclave the residents enjoyed the advantages of life in the country in the middle of urban London. But it was an isolated spot and quite a distance from the nearest transportation facilities.

A round that time my mother arrived in London with my
brother, whom she intended to enroll in a British boarding
school. She took a room in a boarding house which was more conveniently located than the Barneses' house, which was at the bottom of a steep hill and accessible only by a zigzagging footpath
through the grass. She worried about leaving my brother in England while she herself was going back to Germany. I tried my best
to calm her by agreeing with her on everything. One day she announced that Otto L. and his wife were in London on their way to
the Caribbean, and that we must invite them to dinner. Otto was
the stepson of Aunt Else, my grandfather's sister-in-law in Wiesbaden. He was a young physician who was about to emigrate with
his wife, also an M. D., and start a practice in Jamaica. I saw no reason to entertain these non-family strangers whom I had not even
met before. "Perhaps we ought to invite an additional guest," suggested my mother, "somebody who speaks German and is good at
making conversation. Know anybody?" "The only person I can
think of is Peter Drucker," I said. I was not sure at all that he would
want to join us—our romance was in one of its waning stages.

"What!" cried my mother in dismay, "you are still seeing that Austrian?" "Yes, and I am going to telephone him right now." Peter was free and said he would be glad to come.

It had not occurred to either my mother or myself that, before one issues a dinner invitation, one has to make sure that there is food in the house. At home it was the servants' responsibility to see to that. Assuming that the Barneses' pantry had all the required provender, my mother went to her boarding house to rest, and I went down to the kitchen to prepare the food, although I did not know anything about cooking. I found some potatoes and a piece of cheese; I cut up both, layered them in a dish, and put everything into an oven. Never having used the oven—any oven—before, I hoped that everything would turn out all right. Within five minutes there was a shattering noise. The dish, which was not heat-proof, had cracked, and our presumptive dinner had turned into a glutinous mass that stuck to the bottom and the walls of the oven. At that moment Peter arrived. "Help me, help me," I cried, "my mother and our guests are due in ten minutes—what am I going to do?" Alas, it was Sunday night; every store in all of Britain—and Scotland for that matter—was closed. No restaurant was open. We had to improvise. In the pantry we found another potato and a can of sardines which I had overlooked. We divided all that on five plates, and that was our so-called dinner. I mumbled excuses, my mother glowered, Otto and his wife were terribly embarrassed; only Peter kept his good humor.

Our guests left as soon as they could. My mother also decided to depart, postponing her reprimands for my unspeakable negligence until tomorrow when we would be alone. By that time I was an exhausted wreck and unable to respond. Peter offered to escort my mother up the dark path toward her boarding house. While she put her coat on he whispered to me that he would return; he could not bear to see me staying all night by myself in that lonely house, devastated as I was.

He really came back: he put his arms around me and tried to cheer me up while I kept on sobbing and sobbing. Suddenly we heard a loud noise outside, as if a stone was rolling down the hillside. This was followed by loud banging at the door. It was my mother. "Open up," she cried, "I know he's with you." "Wait, I have to find the key," I shouted back, while telling Peter he would have to hide. It would be a catastrophe if she found him here. But where could he go? She would search every room, look under every bed. "The coal cellar," I whispered. "It's the only place she's not likely to go to. I'll lock you in and hide the key." So poor Peter, my gallant swain, spent the better part of the night crouching in a dark cold hole while my mother, as I had anticipated, turned the house upside down trying to find him.

An unbiased spectator would have laughed at the hilarious scenario, which was like a bedroom farce by Feydeau. For me, who was on the spot, it was anything but funny. "I followed him all the way back. I saw him go in," my mother insisted. "From the top of the hill I saw the square of light when you opened the door for him. I knew he'd go back to see you. He's up to no good. And because of you, I fell down. I could not stop myself; I rolled down all the way from the top of the hill. My good suit is ruined. You are going to pay for it! Where is he?" This went on and on till past midnight, when she declared that she would not allow me to stay in the Barneses' house that night. I was going to stay with her at her boarding house. I was so beaten down, I was no longer in a state to protest. Under the pretext that I had to lock up downstairs, I opened the door to the coal cellar and let Peter out through the back door. My mother's room had only one bed; I slept on the floor, or rather, I did not sleep. Her castigations continued throughout the night . . . She was going to disown me. My reply, that I did not care because I was self-supporting, only provoked a new set of lamentation. What a misfortune that one's children nowadays earned enough to disregard their parents' threats of disinheritance. Finally, the ultimate condition for letting up: I must swear, cross my heart, never ever to see Drucker again. If that's what it took to end the harangue I would swear. It would be a mere formality; oaths extorted under pressure are void anyhow.

Next morning, on my way to work, I telephoned Peter: "Please, please, meet me during the lunch hour." I was desperately afraid that the night in the coal cellar had turned him away from me forever. It hadn't. He came to meet me at the Red Lion at Bedford

Square or Russell Square—I remember it was near to the British Museum. He looked remarkably cheerful and dapper, considering the past tribulation. On my part, I had not yet got off the emotional roller-coaster of the past sixteen hours. When he came in the door I was so relieved to see him, I broke down and cried. One of the waitresses, a motherly woman, came to the table. "Sir," she said sternly to Peter, "look, what have you done to that nice young lady? Can't you see how unhappy she is?" And then, turning to me: "Now, don't cry, dearie. I know a good abortionist in Rotherham; you just take the tube, you have to change at Charing Cross, and then . . . " Her well-meant advice struck me as so funny I had to laugh. "Thank you, thank you, but the last thing I need is an abortionist," I told the good woman. She was nonplussed: then what was I crying about?

Yes, what was I really crying about? Peter and I were again together, and that's what really mattered.

When my mother left for Germany a week later, I saw her off at Victoria Station. Waiting for the train to pull out, she leaned out of the open window of her compartment and kept reminding me, who was standing on the platform, of my sworn promise never again to see Peter Drucker, that happy-go-lucky Austrian. As soon as the train started to move, the object of her scorn stepped out from behind a pillar where he had been hiding. We fell into each other's arms.

That was seventy years ago.

In the normal course of events we would have become engaged and set the wedding date—whether the parents approved or not. But we could not get married for another four years. In those Depression years a woman in Great Britain was automatically fired when she got married, in the belief that she would free a spot for an unemployed man. Both Peter and I had good and interesting jobs. I was a market researcher for Marks & Spencer, the fast-growing and innovative retail chain, and Peter was an economist for an investment bank. But at that time wages in England were so low that it would have been very difficult for us to live on Peter's salary alone.

We were young, we fantasized about our future, our marriage and our children—knowing that it was an impossible goal while Hitler was determined to build his Thousand Year Reich at the cost of destroying the world we knew. And we became increasingly oppressed by England's growing bent for appeasing Hitler. In the fall of 1936 we decided to get married and leave for America. Peter's firm gave us a magnificent wedding present: a two weeks' trip, first class, on a cruise ship that was going from Trieste to New York. It was a fantastic honeymoon.

We landed in New York early in 1937 and settled down in a New York suburb. The cost of living was low and we managed to get by. I started a small market research business, and Peter worked as a correspondent for a number of European newspapers. In due course, Peter produced his first two books and I produced our first two children. The tandem schedule continued for the next two books and next two children. Then—after three girls and one boy—I gave up on what turned out to be an unequal collaboration. Peter's output as of this date (2002) amounts to 34 books.

In 1942, five years after we arrived in America, Peter was offered a job as professor at Bennington College in Vermont. We moved at once and became part of a stimulating and quite diverse faculty of that young and ambitious school: the psychologist Erich Fromm, the Dante scholar Francis Ferguson, the dancers and choreographers Martha Graham and José Limon, the writer Shirley Jackson, the architect Richard Neutra, the sociologist Karl Polanyi and many more. We loved living in the country, even during the rigorous winters. I indulged myself by taking all the mathematics and physics courses given at the college—courses I had not been allowed to take ten years earlier. Ultimately, after our return to the New York area, I finally obtained a master's degree in physics from Fairleigh Dickinson University in New Jersey.

After our happy years in Bennington, we moved back to New York in 1949 and bought a house in Montclair, N.J., where we lived for 21 years. The change from the lofty idealism of Bennington to the conformist society of an upper-class suburb was rather startling. I did not have a clue how to behave, what to wear, what to say. I remember my first Parent-Teachers night at the elementary school which my then eight-year-old son attended. A woman came up and told me that she had known the former owner of our house. "Roberta and I were such good friends—we worked on the Bridge together." "Are you an engineer?" I asked. "What makes you think that?" she replied. "Well, you said you worked on a bridge." She looked at me as if I were demented. "The PTA Bridge, that's what I meant."

Peter's life was focused on his teaching at New York University and on consulting assignments all over the country. I think the only person in Montclair with whom he had any affinity and whom he liked to meet was Yogi Berra, the baseball star. I was very much a "soccer mom" and involved in Girl Scouts, Boy Scouts, the PTA, and the Red Cross. But I was looking for a challenge.

I thought I would like to go out for a Ph.D. but I was much too old at the time to become a member of a team doing exciting research. The only work I could expect was in teaching—but that did not attract me. I took a job, first as an editor of science books for a major publisher, and later as an editor and writer for a science encyclopedia. After our youngest child had gone off to college, I answered a help-wanted ad for a technical writer to write patent applications at a patent attorney's office. I took the job and soon after passed the federal exam to become a Registered Patent Agent; I found the work extremely interesting. The inventions I worked on were not all that world shaking. But what fascinated me then—and still does—is the mind of the inventor and the single-minded determination to pursue an idea. Though most of my clients were small time garage-inventors, I had the opportunity at least twice to defend a patent claim before a foreign patent examiner. One of these assignments was at the Japanese Patent Office, where I was probably the first and only foreign woman they had ever seen.

In 1970 Peter had an offer to join the faculty at the Claremont Graduate School, some forty miles east of Los Angeles. After much soul-searching, we accepted and drove across the country in the middle of winter. Claremont, at the foot of the San Gabriel Mountains with its 10,000 foot peaks, has been our home now for over thirty years.

I found a very agreeable working niche as market researcher for manufacturers of high-tech scientific instruments: to identify features which users and, more importantly, potential future users wanted to be incorporated in the respective instruments. I traveled all over the country and sometimes abroad, investigating magnetic resonance imaging devices, marine satellite navigation systems, smog suppressors, electric motors, medical instruments, and printing presses. One job led to another, and even to an invitation to join the board of a Midwestern middle-sized manufacturer of digital oscilloscopes and other highly technical and diverse instruments. I was the only woman on the board, and while the other directors patted themselves on the back for their progressive stance, nobody ever listened to me: "What does SHE know?"

Working as I did, among people who consistently thought of and developed new products, encouraged me to come up with ideas of my own. I applied for a patent for a fast-cooker, which was granted just at the time the microwave oven came on the market. Next, I developed the electronic circuitry for a wristband heart-rate monitor; a cardiologist whom I consulted thought that there was no market for the device. Neither she nor I anticipated the coming aerobic fitness craze and the repeated heart-rate checking during exercise. Discouraged by the opinion of an expert, I abandoned the project, which might—or might not—have become a winner.

As I was getting on in years, I saw my contemporaries succumb to arthritis, osteoporosis, and other "-is" ailments: while I was spared, I developed another affliction: entrepreneuritis. I had bouts of it before, but while I was younger and stronger I could suppress them. Now I just gave in. I had a device in mind which was novel and which was the solution to a common problem. Initial market studies seemed promising. I found a partner, a retired engineer, to supply the hands-on know-how. Together we designed the device, a voice volume monitor, and proceeded past the prototype stage to manufacture. The process proved to be far more demanding than either of us anticipated. Sometimes I ask myself: had I known at the beginning how difficult it would be, would I have pursued my idea? But that is only part of the dilemma. If I had decided not to pursue it, would I have regretted it forever, or what "forever" means to somebody over the age of eighty? My partner has since retired, but I am still running that small business.

"Forever" is also a question I ask myself when it comes to mountain hiking, my favorite recreational occupation. For me, mountain hiking set off sparks of exhilaration at conquering something that looked difficult at the outset. Most of my contemporaries, including Peter, have long given up hiking, but I am still at it, alone or with a group, and people stop me on the trails and ask how old I am. When I tell them, they want to know "how do you do it?"

"How do you do it?" is also a question our children ask. "Sixty-six years of being happily married to the same partner? Incredible."

I stayed in close touch with my mother until she died. She came frequently from London, where she had settled, to visit us and her grandchildren. She grew increasingly fond of Peter, the "despicable Austrian," and, in turn, Peter admired her for her feistiness and her incisive wit. I never got over my fear of her who had so intimidated me during my childhood and adolescence. But after that terrible evening in London at the Barneses' house, she never again tried to dominate or control me.